Breakthrough Networking

Building Relationships That Last

Lillian D. Bjorseth

Second Edition

© 1996, 2003 by Lillian D. Bjorseth

First Printing 1996
Second Printing 2003, revised
Printed in the United States of America

Published by Duoforce Enterprises, Inc.
2221 Ridgewood Rd., PO Box 1154
Lisle IL 60532
630-983-5308; 630-983-5312 (fax)
800-941-3788
lillian@duoforce.com; www.duoforce.com

Publisher's Cataloging-in-Publication Data

Bjorseth, Lillian D.
Breakthrough networking: building relationships that last /
Lillian D. Bjorseth – 2nd edition

     p.   cm.

     Includes bibliographic references and index.
          1.   Business communication
          2.   Interpersonal communication
          3.   Social networks
          4.   Career development
          5.   Public relations
          6.   Success in business

650.13

ISBN 0-9648839-3-7

Dedication

Dedicated to my husband, Wayne Haberlach, who continues to be my strong, supportive behind-the-scenes business and personal partner; and Justin Bjorseth, 5, and Ryan Bjorseth, 2, who already know the value of building a relationship with grandma.

Meet Lillian D. Bjorseth

Lillian Bjorseth makes it easier for entrepreneurs through Fortune 100 employees to meet and get along with others. She helps them improve communication and build healthy relationships as they learn to break the ice and work a room with ease and read and adapt to customers, vendors and co-workers' behavior.

She's known nationally for her infectious enthusiasm and her practical, profound and powerful content that participants can apply immediately whether she is consulting, speaking, training or writing. She helps people enhance communication verbally, nonverbally, in writing and in Cyberspace; present themselves professionally and make professional presentations; and gain top-of-the-mind positioning through strategic networking.

Lillian has the background and experience to walk her talk. A top graduate from the prestigious University of Missouri School of Journalism, she has been communicating throughout her career. At Nicor Gas, she did executive speech writing and public and investor relations. Then it was on to AT&T, where she coached top executives in communication and media relations skills and created and taught her first communication course.

Since 1990, she has put her marketing skills to work for herself and has successfully built Duoforce Enterprises, Inc.

She founded and for 10 years owned Better Business Contacts, a business leads organization that she sold to an international marketing referral company.

She also is the author of *52 Ways To Break The Ice & Target Your Market,* interactive relationship-building tools; and the *Nothing Happens Until We Communicate* audiotape and workbook series. She's a contributing author to *Masters of Networking.*

Lillian is a member of the National Speakers Association and was honored by the Illinois chapter for her "unrelenting enthusiasm and commitment to the speaking profession." She's an adjunct professor for Lewis University's Graduate School of Management and a member of its MBA Executive Advisory Board. She is also a faculty member for North Central College's Entrepreneurship Institute. She's past chair of the Naperville IL Chamber of Commerce's Trainers & Consultants Connection, which cited her for taking the group "from ground zero to a highly respected committee."

Lillian has received numerous awards for her public relations work and authorships. She was named an Influential Woman in Business by the *Business Ledger* and the Chicago Chapter of the National Association of Women Business Owners and is listed in *Who's Who in the Media and Communications, Outstanding People in the 20th Century, 2000 Notable American Women, The Dictionary of International Biography, International Who's Who of Professional and Business Women, The National Registry of Who's Who* and *Who's Who in Executives.*

Lillian is available to help your association members, board of directors and company management and employees build healthier internal and external relationships. Her offerings include keynotes, workshops and in-house and one-on-one consulting and training.

About the Second Edition

I'm delighted that so many people agree that relationship-building is the way to increase sales and enhance career success ... so many, in fact, that we have had to go "back to the presses." It's been heartening to hear from people whose lives we have touched positively, and I look forward to hearing from you, too!

We've retained many of our time-honored communication and networking principles while also refining and adding techniques and tips. The chapter on how to create a Verbal Business Card, based on one of my popular workshops, is a powerful addition to the book and a must-have in your networking toolkit. Those first few sentences you say when meeting new people or getting reacquainted may well be the most important in your repertoire.

My years of training and consulting with tens of thousands of people on the importance of understanding why you act the way you do and how to modify your behavior to be more successful have helped me add new, vital data specially geared to the networking and Cyberspace arenas. While you may have experienced DISC in the workplace, few of you know specifically your strengths and limitations in networking situations, which can be the most stress producing (and often career impacting!) in your business day. Our information can give you the added confidence to create the positive and professional aura you want.

From my 10 years of owning a focused business leads organization, I learned that starting/maintaining meaningful conversations and successfully marketing products and

services are two areas where business people need continuing help. Thus, I created *52 Ways To Break The Ice & Target
Your Market*, a relationship-building product based on two
decks of unique cards, **ICE BREAKERS** and **MARKET
TARGETERS**. Check out Part IV for more information on how
these tools can help you conduct more meaningful and effective meetings, conferences and workshops.

Also, be sure to read about the host and guest responsibilities regarding meal etiquette that we have added since
face-to-face meetings often occur over breakfast, lunch or dinner. And, you want to be sure to do the right thing.

Happy and successful networking!

Contents

Preface

Networking as a way to increase business and career success has become a way of life. It's a buzzword everyone uses; yet few truly know how to do it. *Breakthrough Networking* is all about building and maintaining salient and profitable business relationships. No matter what industry you are in or what level you have reached in your business or career, you can profit from additional professional alliances. Networking can help you start a new business, increase your sales and/or boost your career opportunities through lateral moves or promotions within or outside your company.

Time and money for networking activities need to be a part of your business plan, whether you are marketing yourself, your products or your services. You'll be hard-pressed to succeed in business without networking. It can be done almost anywhere: at the office, on a golf course, at an after-hours event, at an industry conference, on an airplane or a train and through e-mail once you have met someone.

You already experience encounters like these. *Breakthrough Networking* shows you how to turn them into profitable relationships.

Building better business contacts begins within you—the pride you have in yourself. Your self-esteem, self-confidence and love of self will naturally lead people to you. Your acceptance of yourself and your comfort level will make others feel at ease with you.

How you feel about yourself is manifested outwardly in your image, a combination of your appearance and behavior.

People decide when meeting you (sometimes just by seeing you!) if they want to include you in their network or want to be included in yours. In this book, I show you how to look, act and be professional to increase your success at building relationships that last.

A positive image needs to be carried over into your corporate personality—your business cards, letterhead, brochures, sales materials and your website. If you work for someone else, your corporate personality is closely intertwined with your employer. Make sure you are comfortable with the image of the company you choose to work for since it also becomes intertwined with yours.

While a positive image is the first step, you must also have a repertoire of networking skills to build professional alliances. I share with you myriad practical and "political" hints I have experienced and observed in more than 25 years with Fortune 100 companies and as an entrepreneur and founder of two successful companies.

Part I of *Breakthrough Networking* provides an introduction to the networking process and helps you discover your networking behavioral style. Each of us behaves differently; however, there are enough similarities that since the days of Hercules, people have concentrated on explaining behavior in terms of four basic temperaments or styles.

An explanation of the four styles will help you learn why you act, feel and think the way you do about networking and how your behavior helps and hinders your relationship-building process; why some people enjoy walking into a roomful of strangers and others find it a burden; why some people automatically file their business cards upon returning to the office and others just as naturally lose them in the "mess" on their desks.

You'll learn how to capitalize on your networking strengths, minimize your alliance-building limitations and adapt to get along better with others and achieve your personal and professional goals.

Part II discusses the importance of non-gender imaging skills, the science of creating and managing the impression you make on others. You'll learn why color, style and fit of your clothes play a major role in how you are perceived. You'll bone up on body language and learn why understanding its peculiarities is just as important as fluently speaking your native language.

I examine how things like posture, handshakes, gestures, space bubbles, eye contact and seating arrangements play an important role in establishing positive first impressions and maintaining them throughout conversations or conferences.

Part III provides the information you need to turn a chance meeting or a planned encounter into a mutually beneficial business connection. I show you how to set and meet networking goals, prepare your verbal business card, design and use your business cards wisely, work a room, stay in touch, make friends with the media, understand and decode gender differences in communication, network to get or change jobs, connect while on the road and psyche yourself.

Part IV provides you with proven get-acquainted activities you can use to get attendees mingling before and during your meetings and conferences. These ideas, when viewed alone, may not be "breakthrough." When added together, however, the sum will help you "break through" to sell more products and services, find the job you want and catapult and propel you to the top.

Breakthrough Networking will be your constant, friendly companion in the serious business of building lasting relationships.

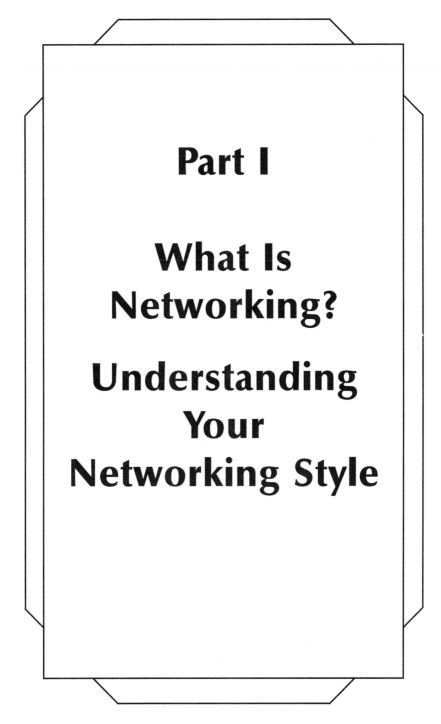

Part I

What Is Networking?

Understanding Your Networking Style

chapter 1

Introduction to Networking

From the beginning, human beings have interacted with one another for psychological, social, business and biological reasons. This kind of associating or relationship building has many names—establishing rapport, developing alliances, networking, partnering, marrying, feeling a kinship—yet all of them share a common goal: to meet personal or professional needs and wants. *Networking* is a relatively new term for the age-old practice of building relationships. The noun turned verb was coined in the 1970s, was popularized in the 1980s and is now a way of life.

It was present in the Garden of Eden with Adam and Eve. We are all proof that *they* connected. When Moses was chosen to lead the children of Israel out of Egypt, he asked God for Aaron's assistance—Aaron, the charismatic communicator and persuasive speaker who helped smooth the way and grease the skids.

Networking in the past often took a different twist—just as it may do today. Remember what happened when reserved Miles Standish asked his outgoing, gregarious friend John Alden to speak to Priscilla in his behalf. The now famous "Why don't you speak for yourself, John?" led to unexpected results.

Cotton Mather, in 1726, advised young men preparing for the ministry in Colonial America to:

> "Form a sodality. What I mean, is, Prevail with a Fit
> Number . . . of Sober, Ingenious and Industrious Young
> Men, to Associate with you, and meet One Evening
> in a Week, for the spending of Two or Three Hours, in
> a Profitable Conversation." (1)

While it is not surprising that the advice in those days was directed toward men, it is disappointing—and somewhat surprising—that men still benefit most from networking in the work place. The old boy network still has the power brokers since men control most of the major corporations in the world.

Women, however, are gaining in numbers what they lack in force. So many of them are starting businesses and becoming owners and presidents that they are beginning to gain clout through sheer numbers. This, in turn, adds clout to the relationships they are building.

Most women are natural networkers. They, their mothers and their grandmothers have been recommending recipes, hairdressers and skin care products across kitchen tables for generations. Many just need to hone these skills for use in the office and on the golf course and put this expertise to work in finding customers and clients for their associates and themselves.

Networking Is a Nongender Skill

Building beneficial relationships knows no gender boundaries. As with any other skill—and networking *is* a skill—it takes knowledge, desire and practice to perfect it.

Some people fail at networking because they don't take time to learn its intricacies, the myriad tips that turn a novice into a master. Far more people fail because they don't start at the beginning—with themselves. Knowledge of yourself— your strengths, limitations, likes, dislikes, hot buttons, your image in person and in print—is vital to being a good networker. Networking without intrapersonal information is like fishing without bait: You may have your hook in the water, but you'll never catch anything.

Networking without intrapersonal information is like fishing without bait: You may have your hook in the water, but you'll never catch anything.

High self-esteem and self-confidence are trademarks of good networkers, and you need both for effective intrapersonal communication. People just naturally gravitate toward others who are comfortable with themselves and can spread that good feeling around.

Effective intrapersonal communication is the first step toward effective interpersonal communication, i.e., your ability to get along with others, to sense how they will react, how they want to be treated and how to establish an environment in which to motivate them. It helps you understand with whom other people would be most comfortable, whose work style would complement or enhance theirs, what referrals they need. It is one thing to refer people to one another; it is the polished professional who knows which two of his/her contacts will naturally mesh and grow into a mutually beneficial relationship.

When you make others feel at ease with you and with people you refer them to, you can realistically expect more satisfying relationships, which, in turn, can lead to more profitable experiences for you, personally and professionally.

Every time you match someone with a need with someone who has a want, you increase your network by two. When those two people mesh well, you increase your network by two *enthusiastic, appreciative* people who will be eager to help you.

Before we take an in-depth look at how you can improve your intrapersonal and interpersonal communication skills, let's examine what networking is.

My Definition

Networking is an active, dynamic process that links people into mutually beneficial relationships.

Active—You cannot sit back and wait to be contacted or approached. *You* have to make it happen!

Dynamic—People, events and information are constantly changing. You have to keep up with your industry, your business, your community, your friends.

A process—Networking is a series of hierarchical actions and interactions that leads to a result, a solution, an answer.

Links—The process connects, bonds and couples people with one another.

Mutually beneficial relationships—People need to mutually profit from the interactions to make it work.

Networking Thaws Phone Calls and Warms Up Prospects

Networking makes it easier for you to call on customers, find a job, get promoted. It opens doors, greases skids, thaws phone calls and warms up prospects.

Networking is not selling!

Networking precedes the sale. It's not what you know, but whom you know that opens a door for you. Once inside, of course, you need to rely on your professionalism, expertise, product and service quality to get the sale. *Breakthrough Networking* concentrates on helping you find the "who" to turn the knob for you.

If Bob Jones were an acquaintance of yours, which call would you respond to more favorably?

> *"I am Tom Smith. Bob Jones recommended that I call you. He told me you are looking for marketing services."*

> *"I'm Tom Smith. I'm calling to tell you about the marketing services we offer."*

Tom took the time to build a relationship with Bob Jones, and that's how he got the recommendaton to call you.

The key is for you, too, to use your time at meetings, conferences and other events to build relationships. Meet as many people as is comfortable for you (your personal comfort level and suggested numbers to meet will be discussed in later chapters) and establish a rapport with them. Then later you can contact them or people they referred you to. No one wants to get hit with your sales pitch at a social hour. Save it until you have established your credibility. Your prospects will be much more likely to turn into customers!

While the "warming up" process may take a little longer, the bottom-line results are so much more fruitful than cold calling. Referrals yield 80 percent more results than cold calls.

Also, the person you have taken time to schmooze will be more likely to refer you or do business with you than the one on whom you immediately "moved in for the kill."

300 x 300

Everyone knows 250 to 500 people on a first-name basis. Consider the people you know—former and current business associates, friends, family, neighbors, former classmates from elementary school through college, your children's friends and their families; fellow club and organization members and the people *they* have introduced you to.

Since totals vary among people, let's assume you know 300 people. And let's further guesstimate that each of these 300 knows at least 300 people. That's 90,000 people you have access to!

Breakthrough Networking helps you develop a plan to reach at least a fraction of these people!

Six Degrees of Separation

You are only six people away from anybody you want to meet anywhere in the world! The proven theory is that if any person were to take the people he/she knew and they were to use the people they know, etc., everyone on earth is just six people away from knowing everyone else. (2)

> *I had heard this theory expounded again and again; however, I spent years unsuccessfully trying to find the source. Then the theory itself came to my rescue. I remembered hearing an ad for a telecommunications company based on "Six Degrees of Separation." I repeatedly called the company's advertising department and, ironically, got voice mail, and no return calls! So I decided to be proactive. I called an acquaintance at the company, someone I had appeared with on a home-based business panel. We had completed step one: We*

knew each other. She diligently made phone call after phone call and several months later tracked down the source and sent me proof. Networking paid off!

My workshop audiences prove again and again that the principle works. (See Chapter 23 for the exercise.) Wide-eyed and exuberant, individuals have rushed up to me to tell me their success stories! Many have received solid leads from people they hadn't even known 10 minutes earlier. The hard part is to get participants to end the exercise so we can go on with the workshop!

One woman who sells medical supplies had been try- ing for years to get her foot in the door at a certain hospital. It turned out three of the five people at her table at a chamber of commerce breakfast meeting knew doctors at that hospital and offered to make a phone call for her.

Another person who sells nutritional products wanted contacts in the Asian-American market because her company was expanding overseas. Someone at her table offered to take her as a guest to an Asian-American chamber of commerce meeting.

A printing salesman returned to his seat in the front row with a look of disbelief. He exclaimed, "Lillian, I have a new client. Look, I have his name, company, phone number and what he needs. I can't believe it."

Believe it! The key to this theory and much of networking is that we have to be proactive. We need to tell people what we need and want before they can help us fulfill those de- sires. In my workshops, I show people step-by-step how to make the process work.

I first tried this exercise during the 1992 presidential elec- tion. I was only a person away from knowing two of the three presidential candidates: I went to college with someone who is a partner in Hillary Clinton's former law firm; and, from my corporate days, I have a friend who had worked with Ross Perot several years before his candidacy. It was a little surprising to me at how "close" I was to the candidates.

In Chapters 11 and 19, we give you suggestions on how to prepare an in-depth list of whom you know, and whom *they* know. Chapter 11 is particularly helpful in deciding what clubs and organizations to join. The other one is specifically geared to job hunting.

Networking Opportunities Are Ubiquitous

You can network almost any place any time. Only your creativity limits your possibilities. In addition to the obvious work-related events, chances to cultivate business exist over the backyard fence, at weddings and family gatherings, when shopping—even when waiting in line.

> *Mike, a desktop publisher, told me that one day at the post office he observed a women in line behind him holding a stack of newsletters. When she came outside, he introduced himself and offered to give her a reasonable quote on producing those newsletters. She agreed, and Mike got the job.*

Mike was observing one of the cardinal rules in networking: Anyone within three feet of you is a prospect for your product/service.

My favorite personal experience happened when I was discussing some packaging issues with the printer for my *52 Ways To Break The Ice & Target Your Market* relationship-building product.

> *We met in a hotel lobby near her office where I was waiting to join someone for lunch. I was agreeing with her that her solution was plausible but that it was more*

expensive and less attractive than I had envisioned. A man came over to us and said politely, "Forgive me, but I overheard your conversation and wondered if I might give you my card. I'm in the packaging business!" I looked at him, formed a positive first impression, and replied, "Yes." Turns out he lives near me and did have a creative solution that I bought. Further, he gave me two program leads for associations he belongs to and introduced me to the head of educational services in the home office of a Chicago-area Realtor, who is now considering me to present relationship-building programs.

Use your common sense. If someone scowls at you, appears unwilling to talk or gives a short, curt reply ... back off. Some people may think you are invading their personal space (more on this in Chapter 7). Honor their right to think so. Others, however, may use the opportunity to talk your ear off. **You** may end up getting sold.

When I still owned my business leads organization, I received a cold call from a financial planner. While I was not in need of his services, I noted his sales skills, enthusiasm and dedication. When he was finished with his pitch, I said, "Do I have something for you! I own a networking organization called Better Business Contacts, and it helps you increase your business through word-of-mouth referrals. It can help eliminate cold calls like this." A short time later, he started a new chapter for me!

Networking Is an Art and a Skill

Webster verifies that networking qualifies as an art: "A branch of learning; a skill acquired by experience, study or observation." And, from the same source, it qualifies as a science: "Knowledge attained through study or practice."

Many people learn networking skills informally, even haphazardly. To be most effective, the skill needs to be taught in credit and noncredit courses just as other communication and marketing skills are taught at schools across the country. I currently teach a "Building Healthy Business Relationships" course in a university graduate school of management and in a college entrepreneurship institute. The response from students has been excellent.

Corporations need to include relationship-building courses in their curriculum, both as orientation for new employees because it can save hundreds of hours in aggregate as new employees try to figure out who's who and where to go for what, and as an ongoing program for seasoned employees. (A sampling of the benefits of networking for changing/keeping jobs is provided in Chapter 19.)

With new employees, the fault is not with not knowing; the fault is not being told whom to ask or that it is okay to ask! The cost to the company is the time and money lost as new employees must reinvent the wheel again and again—at the company's expense.

Corporations and colleges need to add relationship-building courses to their curriculum.

It can also be beneficial for seasoned employees.

> *A Fortune 500 company called me when they wanted to send about 50 engineers to a conference and tradeshow. The manufacturing company believed (correctly!) that it would be helpful for the normally more reserved engineers to have more insight into working a room and building relationships ... to benefit themselves and the company.*

> *In addition to skill building, we also assigned "tasks" to the engineers based on the conference programs listed in an advance brochure, i.e., people were assigned to attend certain programs and visit certain booths … with accountability to the conference manger upon return. On the way to the conference in the company-rented bus, the manager also facilitated a review of relationship-building skills based on my materials. It was a major win for the employees and the company, which felt it got a good return on its investment.*

Networking in Cyberspace

When Gen. Israel Putnam was commanding the Revolutionary Army at the Battle of Bunker Hill, he said: "Men, you are all marksmen—don't one of you fire until you see the whites of their eyes."

Using a different twist to that quote, I believe that the best relationships are built when you can see the whites of another's eyes. The World Wide Web can provide a plethora of information about individuals and companies and can be used productively before and after you have met someone. *It can never replace a face-to-face meeting and should be used extremely cautiously for beginning relationships.*

Since the advent of the Internet, people have repeatedly approached me about joining web-based leads groups and have questioned why I didn't start one myself. Neither are plausible methods for building relationships.

First and foremost, we have no guarantee that people are representing themselves honestly and with integrity. That may also be true for people you meet in person and see repeatedly, but the chances are far slimmer that it would happen. This is especially true when you hone your people-reading skills (through the use of DISC and the interpretation of body language, which we discuss later in detail) and you know what to look for when you see the "whites of their eyes."

If, heaven forbid, you were to rely solely on e-mail or chat room communication, you could not even be sure of people's gender or that they are even in the business they purport to be or produce/sell the products or services they promise.

On the positive side, e-mail can be an excellent way to maintain a relationship because it offers immediacy and ease not found in telephone or more formal written communication. The key is to use it professionally and as an adjunct to building and maintaining relationships. See Chapter 16 for how to communicate more effectively in Cyberspace.

We're ready now to start the process of building more profitable relationships by beginning at the beginning—with intrapersonal communication and an introduction to the four styles of behavioral theory.

chapter 2

Introduction to Four Styles of Behavioral Theory

E ach of you has a way you go about meeting your needs, a way that is comfortable for you to act and react when communicating with your co-workers, families and friends.

Your days flow more smoothly, and you feel less stressed and hassled when you can spend most of your time behaving in your natural, comfortable, preferred style. Of course, the best way to ensure this would be to become a hermit so no one could interrupt your ebb and flow.

However, interacting with others is an integral part of being human—and of conducting business. It's imperative that you communicate to ascertain your customers' and clients' needs and wants, so you, in turn, can fulfill them better than anyone else.

And, therein lays the rub.

People in your company, your family and others you want to build relationships with may be comfortable meeting their needs in different ways than you are. They, for instance, might be more people-oriented and want to engage in small talk when you call them. You, on the other hand, may be more task-oriented and want to get right down to business.

Some people may be fast-paced and make decisions quickly. You may like to deliberate and analyze until you feel you have exhausted all possible avenues and consequences and are assured you have made the best possible choice. In fact, you may be irked by people who act too quickly and may make unnecessary mistakes.

The differences in pace and priority pose real problems in relationship building. You really want to get Tom's business; however, his need to discuss every aspect of the Chicago Bears' recent win before discussing the matter at hand makes you want to pull your hair (maybe even his!) out.

Alan, on the other hand, has given you only $1,000 worth of business for the year. Yet, you would much rather take him to lunch because you like being around him. You just naturally are on the same wavelength. He seems to know just how much sports talk you like. Your blood pressure doesn't rise one degree when you are with him!

Much of this comfort or discomfort can be traced to natural behavioral styles, which history shows generally fall into four styles or temperaments. The first mention is in Greek mythology, (3) when, according to legend, Zeus empowered four gods to make man more god-like:

1. **Apollo**—to give spirit
2. **Dionysus**—to give joy
3. **Epimetheus**—to give sense of duty
4. **Prometheus**—to give scientific thought

Around 450 BC, Greek physicians Hippocrates and Galen wrote about four basic temperaments and their belief that these temperaments were determined by the type of "humor" or body fluid that dominated a person's internal composition:

1. **Choleric**—yellow bile: quick to act, determined, easily angered

2. **Sanguine**—blood: optimistic, outgoing, warm-hearted, volatile

3. **Phlegmatic**—phlegm: calm, patient, slow to act

4. **Melancholic**—black bile: anxious, quiet, serious

This theory remained popular throughout the Middle Ages. The temperaments were considered mutually exclusive, i.e., an individual possessed only one of them.

Psychologist Wilhelm Wundt, recognized as the founder of experimental psychology, theorized around the mid-20th century that people possess degrees of two characteristics: quickness/slowness and strength/weakness. He abandoned the earlier exclusivity theory by saying it was possible to have both in varying degrees.

Soon thereafter, Dr. Carl Jung espoused the theory that people have one of two basic personality orientations—introverted or extroverted. He said that both are present: one of them dominant and conscious, the other subordinate and unconscious. He cited four basic psychological functions: thinking, feeling, sensing and intuiting. Jung postulated that differences in behavior result from preferences in using different functions to meet our needs. He believed they emerge early in life and form the foundation for our personalities. (4)

Katharine C. Briggs and her daughter Isabel Briggs Myers used Jung's work as the foundation for their personality measurement tool, the Myers-Briggs Type Indicator.

When William Marston published *The Emotions of Normal People* in 1928, he was the first to identify the four behavioral styles as dynamic and situational. In his introduction to the condensed version of Marston's book, Dr. John Geier says that:

> "... one individual could possess many traits and that the intensity of traits within the person might indicate a difference in behavior." (5)

It was not until the mid-1950s that further developments emerged in the four style theories. One that is relevant here is Dr. Geier's work at the University of Minnesota. Adapting a list of adjectives Marston had used to describe the different styles, Geier developed the Personal Profile System®*, which is published by Inscape Publishing Inc.

I have found the Personal Profile System with its DiSC®* Dimensions of Behavior to be the most user-friendly instrument to help explain the four styles of behavior and the impact they have on everyone's personal and professional lives. Because the assessment tool is self-administered, self-scored and provides immediate results, it is easy to use and a powerful tool for relationship building in personal, sales, social and work situations. We have had extraordinary results with individuals for personal growth and within companies and organizations when used for management and professional development.

In the next chapter, we will take an in-depth look at the four behavioral styles and how they relate to relationship building and increasing your business. We will build on this foundation throughout the book to increase your knowledge of behavioral styles and to show you the importance and relevance of using this information in your work, your personal life and your social life.

*Registered trademark of Inscape Publishing Inc.

chapter 3

Your Networking Style Quiz

E ach of you is as unique as a snowflake. Like snowflakes, you also have similarities, enough so that we can group behavioral characteristics into four major categories. Each of you exhibits varying amounts of all of them. Most of you have the tendency to show dominance in one or more categories, i.e., this is the behavior or behaviors you feel comfortable exhibiting.

Most of you also exhibit a low amount of certain behavioral characteristics, i.e., you prefer not to act in a certain way when you have a choice. It is not natural or comfortable for you.

Through knowledge of your behavioral style, you will get a better understanding of your strengths and limitations. You will know your hot buttons: what makes you tick and why you act, react, feel and think the way you do. What is it that makes you "you"? How can you become a better "you"? In what situations are you most effective? In what environments are you least effective? With the answers to these questions, you can purposefully seek out personal and professional opportunities where you are naturally most effective and increase your changes for success and happiness. Conversely, you can seek to eliminate or lessen the amount of time you need to spend in environments least conducive to your communication style.

> *My friend Jennifer is a creative type and excels at looking at the big picture and literally spouting out ideas by the dozens. She functions best when she is surrounded by people who inspire her creativity and even write down her ideas as they flow.*
>
> *On numerous occasions, she has mentioned to me that she is feeling sluggish, and is frustrated with her business. Each time, we have analyzed her current projects and have found that she was caught up in detail, like inputting brochure copy, proofing it and trying to get it properly aligned for the printer ... rather than creating the copy.*
>
> *Jennifer does not have a lot of patience nor does she like detail work. She does not function well when she needs to implement all the aspects of her wonderfully creative ideas.*
>
> *We helped her solve that dilemma. She hired an assistant who loves detail work and following instructions.*

Once you have improved your intrapersonal communication, i.e., you are comfortable with who you are and, preferably, really like who are, you can use the same model to improve interpersonal communication.

What makes other people tick? Why do they act or react the way they do? What kind of environment motivates them? Based on that knowledge, how can you act to reduce conflict, strengthen relationships and increase productivity and bottom line results? You will quickly find that, to get the best results, you will have to adapt to different kinds of behavior among family members and the people who work with you. It helps explain the perennial questions:

◆ "Why do my two children react so differently when I ask both of them to do the same chore?

◆ "Why is one of my employees so much more productive and satisfied than the other? After all, I treat them the same."

"The same" is the key. It is unrealistic for you to expect other people to behave the same way you do or the same as other people. What is realistic, and possible, is to better understand why you and they behave and communicate the way you do.

When you know more about why you have the tendency to behave the way you do than the other person understands about behavioral or communication styles, you will be ahead of the game. When you also understand more about why others behave as they do, you will be charge of the situation.

The only person you can control is yourself. When you want/need people to behave differently—like getting them to close a sale or recommend you to another person—you need to change *your* behavior. When you know how to make other people feel more comfortable (people like being dealt with in their style), you can realistically expect better results. It will signal the beginning of more satisfying professional and personal relationships as well as more sales and career success.

The model we will use to help you discover your networking style is *DISC*, which stands for:

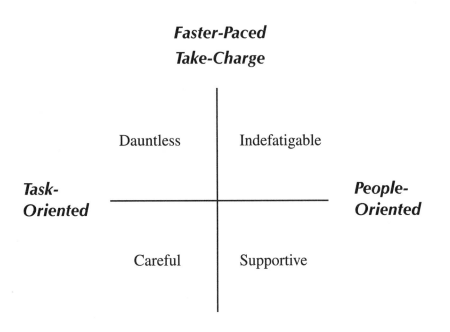

- ◆ Dauntless
- ◆ Indefatigable
- ◆ Supportive
- ◆ Careful

It's time to find out your networking style(s). It will be fun—and rewarding!

Learn Your Networking Style

1. In each of the sets of four statements, identify those behaviors that are typically *most* or *least* characteristic of you. Read the four statements under each heading, then rank them from 4 to 1, giving a 4 to the behavior most like you, 3 to the next most like you, then 2, with 1 being the statement that reflects your least typical behavior.

2. Beginning with the "A" statements, enter the number you assigned to each in the appropriate box on page 29. Repeat the process for all "B," "C" and "D" statements.

3. Check your accuracy by adding the columns together; they will equal 150. If they don't, recheck to make sure you have attributed all four numbers in each scenario.

4. Look at the answer key on page 30 to verify your most prevalent networking style(s). If two of the numbers are the same, you have a tendency to use both of these styles equally.

Appearance

A. I always wear power suits and accessories when I attend any business function.

B. I usually wear suits; however, I like to deviate from the gray / navy blue syndrome and individualize with accessories that have panache. I have to be me!

C. I like to blend into the crowd. Gray or taupe slacks or skirt and a navy blazer make me feel comfortable.

D. I prefer conservative, tailored clothes and accessories, and everything needs to be perfect, down to the last detail.

Business Card Filing System

   A. I only save those for which I have an immediate need.

   B. I have more fun collecting business cards than using them. I have yet to develop a filing system so I may find cards in the darnedest places.

   C. I date all my cards in the upper right-hand corner and file them alphabetically by company name.

   D. I collect a limited amount, and I know when and where I got each of them.

Cars

   A. Cadillacs or BMWs are for me.

   B. Corvettes or sports cars, in general, are my choice!

   C. Standard SUVs are so practical for business and family.

   D. Reading *Consumer Reports* is a must for me before I buy a car.

Correspondence

   A. I like it brief and informal . . . if I write at all.

   B. I use lots of exclamation points and underlines to show my enthusiasm.

   C. Sincerity and warmth are my goals.

   D. I like formality. I often add attachments for more clarity.

Desktops

A. I like to delegate to others so I can keep routine items off my desk and work on the really big things.

B. I haven't seen the top of my desk since I bought it. In fact, I frequently use the floor for filing.

C. I file things as soon as I am done with them. I also keep my "pending" files updated.

D. My desktop may look messy; however, I know where *everything* is.

Facial Expressions

A. I maintain direct eye contact. I show impatience when people don't get to the point quickly.

B. I have lively, animated facial expressions. I show my feelings, and since I am optimistic, I like to share my enthusiasm with everyone I meet.

C. I have a friendly, warm smile. It's hard to get me perturbed.

D. I don't like people to know what I am thinking; I am comfortable being called stoic.

Goals

A. I have one goal—to get immediate results in everything I do and to eliminate anything that stands in my way.

B. My goals? They're in my head. I haven't had a chance to write them down yet.

C. I set them in December for the following year. Then, I type and file them by month in a 12-part folder.

D. I do thorough short- and long-term planning to help ensure success.

Handshakes

    A. I shake hands firmly and with a purpose.

    B. I am often so busy speaking with my hands I forget to even shake.

    C. I am known for my warm handshake. It can be firm, but mostly I want people to feel my sincerity.

    D. My handshakes are formal. I do it more because of society dictates than because I want to. I don't particularly like being touched.

Information Gathering

    A. I hire somebody to do my research. I get irritated when they don't deliver on time.

    B. I need to concentrate on this area more. I often fire before I aim.

    C. I budget time in the library and on the web in the weekly schedule I set on Sundays.

    D. It is imperative that I have all the data before I make a decision. I take whatever time I need to get it.

Listening

    A. I listen best when what the speaker says fits my agenda. I like people to get to the bottom line quickly.

    B. It's hard for me to listen. I have so much to say.

    C. I try to understand what others are saying and pay attention even if I am not that interested. I don't want to hurt their feelings.

    D. I assess what is being said and listen for consistency. I carefully control my responses.

Making an Entrance

A. People "feel" when I enter a room. My confident posture contributes to a powerful aura.

B. I usually add excitement when I enter a room. I enjoy being in the spotlight.

C. I often slip into a room unnoticed and remain in the background.

D. I pride myself in observing more than being observed.

Office Enhancements

A. I proudly show off my awards and trophies.

B. I like to show off photographs of me and business associates and inspirational posters. I never have enough space!

C. Family photographs make me feel warm and fuzzy.

D. I like to display my diplomas, certificates and credentials in an unassuming way.

Phone Calls

A. This is John. I'll pick you up at noon. We're going to Joe's Eatery.

B. Hi! Isn't the weather lovely? I had the greatest weekend.

C. Hi, this is Bonnie. Is this a good time for you?

D. Hello, this is Mrs. Jones. I'm following up as promised in my April 10 letter.

Reading a Newspaper

A. I read the business advice column first so I know *what* the latest networking/sales techniques are.

B. I read the personal profiles first so I know *who* is important to know.

C. I read the entire newspaper, starting on page one. I like orderliness, and I read the paper *how* it was assembled.

D. I write the editor whenever I find a grammatical or factual error. I want to know *why* it was allowed to happen.

Sales Calls

A. I am brief, clear and to the point. I keep small talk to a minimum.

B. I view it as a social interaction. If the client wants me there, I'll spend as much time as necessary.

C. I establish rapport with a customer. I patiently listen and give personal assurances.

D. I use a logical approach, with plenty of backup data.

Answer Key

	A Dauntless	B Indefatigable	C Supportive	D Careful
Appearance				
Business Card Filing System				
Cars				
Correspondence				
Desktops				
Facial Expressions				
Goals				
Handshakes				
Information Gathering				
Listening				
Making an Entrance				
Office Enhancements				
Phone Calls				
Reading a Newspaper				
Sales Calls				
Total				

Totals will equal 150.

- ◆ If your highest number is in Column A, you are a *Dauntless Networker.*

- ◆ If your highest number is in Column B, you are an *Indefatigable Networker.*

- ◆ If your highest number is in Column C, you are a *Supportive Networker.*

- ◆ If your highest number is in Column D, you are a *Careful Networker.*

Some of you will find you clearly prefer one style above the rest. Others will find two styles that are nearly equal. In that case, you feel comfortable exhibiting either style and let the situation dictate. Still others will find a tendency to prefer three styles equally, and a much smaller percentage will find a nearly equal distribution among all four styles. If you would like more specific information on behavioral styles, contact the author or use the order form in this book. Turn to the next chapter to find out more about your networking *modes operandi.*

A Close-Up Look at the Four Networking Styles

And, now, for the moment of truth! It's time to find out what your answers indicate about you and your relationship-building tendencies.

The first two styles, Dauntless and Indefatigable, are naturally more assertive, fast-paced, outgoing and take-charge people. They find it easier and more comfortable to meet and network with others. The other two styles, Supportive and Careful, tend to be introspective, pensive, quiet and slower-paced. These reserved people usually find relationship building much more difficult, even a necessary burden at times.

You may be a combination of several styles and find yourself exhibiting different behaviors at networking events. If you are nearly equal Indefatigable and Careful styles, you may be at ease and really enjoy certain events; other times you would rather be alone or may become irritated if the meeting is not organized and orchestrated to your high standards. You need to recognize and adjust to differences inside yourself just as you recognize and adjust to differences among people.

It is also important to note that your behavior in networking situations may vary from that you exhibit in other business and social circumstances. That's why I specifically created the networking applications. Many people are assessed in their roles as employees, managers and team members as part of their management development program. Yet these people never know how they naturally behave as "networkers," a process so vital to business and career success and among the most stress-producing situations you experience in your professional career!

We'll take an over-all look at each style before zeroing in on networking specifics.

The Dauntless Networker

We'll look at the "Ds" first—for good reason. People with this style are the most impatient and quickly lose interest in anything that is not directly related to them or their bottom line.

You, the Dauntless Networker, rush in where mere mortals fear to tread! No matter that you are a low-level supervisor and the other meeting attendees are top-level managers. You dislike corporate hierarchies and try to sidestep them. You relish being number one even if your company has only one employee.

If you are an entrepreneur, no one will ever know the business you have been operating for two years has yet to make a profit! Your confidence and presence assure people you are successful!

Your high sense of self-worth contributes to the risk-taking, love of adventure and competitive nature necessary to get your own business off the ground. If you work for some-one else, you definitely need authority along with responsi-bility. You may become restless, bored and eager to break away from the corporate scene. A "rightsizing" may well be the answer to your prayers. You can *finally* do your own thing.

Your shortcoming may be that you probably will not do a business plan first. Your high ego worth, in your mind, in-sures that if you hang out a shingle, the world will come to your doorstep.

This is not necessarily true. You need to do a plan or hire someone to do it for you. You need to market your services. *You need to network!* Don't let your sense of "knowing it all" hinder your relationship building. You need to guard against sharing so many me-me-me stories and how much you have accomplished. Keep on that path, and you'll find people try-ing to avoid you or make a quick getaway in business and social situations.

You have a powerful aura, and it accompanies you wher-ever you go. At networking events, people feel your pres-ence when you walk into a room. At meetings, you let people know your opinions. Others know you are someone to reckon with.

**You have a powerful aura,
and it accompanies you wherever you go.**

You have the choice whether to use that awesome leadership ability for the good of yourself and others, or to run slipshod over people as you try to fulfill your personal ambitions.

Motivated by bottom-line results, the Dauntless style shows impatience in person, on the phone, at conferences. Known for interrupting people, tapping pencils and feet—

alternately or simultaneously—and blunt, quick comebacks, you often turn "off" as many people as you turn "on." You thrive on directness (let's get to the bottom line—give it to me straight) and feel comfortable interacting in the same manner.

You are good at getting results. What others question is how you accomplish them. Be more considerate of other people's feelings, and the sky is the limit for you.

An appropriate sign above your desk is:

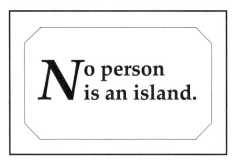

No person is an island.

Let's look at your specific networking strengths, limitations, suggestions for improvements (yes, there are some!) and how others can more effectively build relationships with you.

Relationship-Building Strengths

- ◆ Confident—
  - Exhibits powerful aura
  - Expands to fit space
  - Maintains steady eye contact
  - Shakes hands firmly
  - Uses strong, forceful gestures
- ◆ Decisive—sets own schedule
- ◆ Direct—gives short, pointed description of self/work

- Efficient—uses time wisely
- Fearless—meets strangers with ease
- Independent—attends alone, makes up own mind
- Practical—sorts through the fluff and gets to the meat
- Take-charge—
  - Introduces self to others
  - Introduces people to each other

Relationship-Building Limitations

- Biting—has a sharp-edged tongue
- Blunt—hurts others through insensitivity to feelings
- Domineering—takes over conversations/event itself if there's an opening; may even try to do so without an opening
- Impatient—
  - Dislikes small talk
  - Finishes others' sentences
  - Gets bored easily
  - Interrupts others
  - Judges events too quickly
  - Lets eyes wander around the room
  - Looks at watch
  - Talks over others
  - Twitches
- Inattentive—disregards details like people's names and other relevant information

Suggestions for Improvement

◆ Accept event etiquette and protocol ... even when you don't agree.

◆ Accept that every networking event may not yield immediate results.

◆ Allow others to come to their own conclusions.

◆ Ask questions as if you really care about the answer.

◆ Count to three before you speak to ensure the other person is finished.

◆ Follow up and say thanks.

◆ Identify with a group/organization; become part of a team.

◆ Listen even if the outcome doesn't personally affect you.

◆ Realize you need other people.

◆ Refrain from trying to run the conversation, the event, the meeting or the project.

Strategies for Networking Most Effectively With Dauntless People

◆ Be prepared for quick topic changes or incomplete sentences.

◆ Be sure of information you share; you may be questioned.

◆ Challenge them to help accomplish goals.

◆ Don't take the brusque, blunt style personally!

◆ Give brief answers; save the details for others.

◆ Keep the encounter short, meaningful.

◆ Listen carefully; you may learn from their creative, visionary outlook.

◆ Look them in the eye.

◆ Set up another meeting to continue conversation/sales pitch.

◆ Shake hands firmly.

◆ Show need for and advantages of teamwork.

◆ Show results—help solve their challenges.

◆ Stand up for your rights (you deserve to be treated equally).

◆ Stick to business, current events, sports; avoid personal disclosure issues.

◆ Stick to logic.

Example of a Dauntless Networker

Ben questions his boss's recommendation that he attend the state meeting of the sales and marketing organization of which he is a member. He has at least a dozen sales calls to make. Besides, he isn't sold on this "networking" hype. He has yet to personally experience its effectiveness as a marketing tool.

Can the people at the meeting really help him meet his annual sales goals? Does he need them? How will they contribute to his bottom line?

Ben believes his success so far is due largely to his own efforts. He is forceful and knows when to take action. After all, he sold that bank president whom everyone said could not be convinced.

"I'll go," Ben tells his boss "with the caveat that if I don't find it relevant I can leave after the first day. It doesn't take me long to make a decision."

The Indefatigable Networker

Webster's definition of "indefatigable" describes this style perfectly:

"… incapable of being fatigued; untiring."

Networking was designed for you, the Indefatigable Networker! You find it delightful and entertaining. You can't get enough. Heaven for you is a roomful of people—and an invitation to enter. After-hours events that last for an hour or two are far too short because you have so many people to greet and so much to say to each of them.

**Heaven for you is a roomful of people—
and an invitation to enter.**

You were born schmoozing! You won the hearts of the doctors and nurses before you left the hospital! You are like a kid in a candy store when you attend a cocktail party or conference: so many people to talk with and so little time. How do you choose among all these potential friends and customers?

The point is moot. You strike up a conversation in the parking lot, in the elevator, in the registration line and already are in the swing before you get both feet inside the room.

Your love of meeting and talking with people can also be a detriment: You need to guard against getting so carried away with your stories that you meet only a few people. Your desire to be on center stage leads to storytelling rather than information-gathering.

Or you may feel the urge to meet everyone and, in your breathless race to do so, barely get to know anyone. I have seen Indefatigables leave events with at least 50 business cards, each one obtained one-on-one!

Learning comes from listening. Pay attention to what others know and need and want: It's key to building relationships and selling yourself, your product or service. Learn to benefit from others' experiences, knowledge and expertise.

An appropriate sign above your desk is:

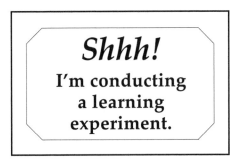

Shhh!
**I'm conducting
a learning
experiment.**

Relationship-Building Strengths

- Animated—keeps people entertained, involved through lively, vivacious behavior

- Enthusiastic—creates excitement for any event ... before, during and after

- Friendly—makes people feel welcome

- Optimistic—makes best out of who and how many attend and believes everything happens for a reason

- Persuasive—convinces others to attend and participate

- Promoting—functions like a public relations machine

- Spontaneous—turns on a dime if event/project needs shot in the arm

- Stimulating—inspires others to mix and mingle

- Trusting—believes people are basically good and honest

- Untiring—uses seemingly boundless energy to organize, direct and follow through

Relationship-Building Limitations

- Animated—talks with hands ... that need to remain void of food and drink

- Disorganized—loses business cards, forgets events and to follow through with thank you calls/notes

- Emotional—reacts from heart rather than head

- Idealist—becomes overly optimistic about networking results

- Incessant talker—gets on others' nerves and even exhausts people

- Manipulative—"cons" people into following them

- Sensitive—Gets hurt easily by what others feel and say

- Unstructured—

  - Forgets business cards, or can't find them amongst all that have been collected

  - Gets address/date/time wrong

  - Overstays welcome

  - Shows up late

  - Vain—needs to be on center stage, even when others have earned the right to be there

Suggestions for Improvement

- Analyze what others have said before you reply.

- Ask open-ended questions. Then be quiet and focus on the answers.

- Balance natural people orientation with more task-directed behavior, and do what you promise.

- Become more succinct verbally and in writing ... get to the point.

◆ "Do it" rather than discuss how it is "to be done."

◆ Force yourself to listen at least 75% of the time.

◆ Keep a back-up supply of business cards in your briefcase and glove compartment.

◆ Make at least minimal notes on others' business cards to aid your recall.

◆ Network strategically vs. just attending events.

◆ Pay more attention to details.

◆ React logically vs. emotionally.

◆ Research the facts.

◆ Show up on time, prepared and at the right place.

◆ Take a time management course.

◆ Wait your turn!

Strategies for Networking Most Effectively With Indefatigable People

◆ Ask about them and their business.

◆ Ask them to lead an activity, announce door prizes, draw names for raffles.

◆ Avoid confrontations and win-lose situations.

◆ Be animated in your responses.

◆ Compliment them.

◆ Give them an opportunity to verbalize.

◆ Handle the details.

◆ Have a planned "exit" statement in person and on the phone.

◆ Help keep them on track.

◆ Interrupt and talk over them, as a last resort.

- Learn from their natural networking style.

- Let them share or have center stage.

- Offer to connect them with VIPs (they will love you forever).

- Tell them who else successfully uses your product/ service.

Example of an Indefatigable Networker

Jane can hardly wait to pack her suitcases. She is so excited that the company is sending her to Las Vegas to work its booth at one of the largest computer trade shows in the industry.

"Just think of all the people I'll get to meet," she tells Betty. "Thousands of people will come to the booth every day. Think of all the business cards I'll have to sort through when I get back. Want to come over for coffee and help me?

"I won't get much sleep, that's for sure—with the casinos and all the great shows. I hear that some hotels serve a breakfast special all night long. Think I'll take a client to breakfast at 3 AM! I've never done that before.

"I gotta run. I have seven more people to call, and it's already 10 PM. I'll talk to you the minute I get back."

The Supportive Networker

A quiet, even-handed, steady approach pervades throughout your networking activities. You are known for the calming effect you have on others. Your sincerity is evident through your handshake, your smile and your demeanor.

Supportive networkers are the best listeners. Your "Tell me more," "Go on," and "What do you think?" prompts encourage others to open up to you and make them feel important. When cornered by Indefatigables, you find it difficult to break away even if you want to ... and they unabashedly take advantage of you!

Supportive networkers are the best listeners.

You don't want to knowingly hurt anyone's feelings. You tend to be uncomfortable when the conversation heats up and would rather withdraw into your shell until any conflict blows over. If, however, you think you may be the cause of any ill feelings, you will approach the person to smooth things over.

Preferring the security of warm, friendly relationships, you like to avoid the unknown. Yet, as a Supportive-style business owner or employee, you are cognizant of the benefits of networking and know you occasionally have "to take the plunge." Your compromise is to seek a safe environment, which may mean talking to the same person for most of the event. As one of my Supportive friends says:

> *"It feels good. When I find someone I am comfortable with, I stay with him or her so I don't have to venture into the unknown again. Getting up the courage to attend is venturesome enough. I prefer to work in a booth at a trade show. It gives me a safe place to call home."*

Ask your outgoing friends to take you under their wings and include you as they comfortably glide through the crowd. Learn by watching and experiment at your own pace next time. It's okay to talk with only two people at an event; however, it's also good for you to set a goal to slowly work that number up to three or four people!

A comforting sign above your desk is:

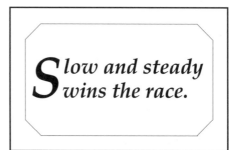

S low and steady wins the race.

Relationship-Building Strengths

♦ Amicable—welcomes people warmly in a low-key manner

♦ Calm—

- Exhibits pleasant facial expressions

- Gives gentle, yet meaningful, handshake

- Makes eye contact that is comfortable for both parties

- Soothes excited, upset people

♦ Considerate—

- Listens patiently

- Makes sure people are comfortable in their surroundings

- Remembers people's names and other relevant information

- Responds thoughtfully

♦ Cooperative—flows with the consensus to keep peace and harmony

♦ Deliberate—has a relationship-building plan and carefully and methodically executes it

♦ Dependable—

- Fulfills obligations as promised
- Is loyal, almost to a fault
- Keeps confidences
- Shows up on time or early
- Steadies/stabilizes a relationship
- Values trustworthiness in others

◆ Genuine—acts sincerely and honestly ... what you see is what you get

◆ Modest—gives credit to team/group/others

◆ Supportive—believes in mutually beneficial relationships

Relationship-Building Limitations

◆ Fixed—dislikes unforeseen forks in the road

◆ Follower—waits indefinitely for people to approach them

◆ Noncompetitive—gives in to maintain harmony

◆ Sensitive—takes criticism personally

◆ Structured—

  - Likes sameness in agenda, meeting location, number of attendees
  - Wrestles with sudden, unexpected change

◆ Timid—dislikes ... really dislikes ... walking into roomful of strangers

◆ Uncertain—

  - Doubts they can stand own turf
  - Is overwhelmed by Dauntless or Indefatigable networkers on a roll

◆ Wishy-washy—tries to please everyone

Suggestions for Improvement

- ◆ Attend at least two networking functions a month.
- ◆ Make yourself act like a host vs. a guest at least once at every event.
- ◆ Practice and polish your presentation skills before live audiences.
- ◆ Set reachable goals (meet two or three new people at an event) and pat yourself on the back.
- ◆ Stand up for your rights.
- ◆ Take an assertive training course ... twice!
- ◆ Vary your agenda slightly to get more comfortable with change.
- ◆ Venture into new surroundings; meet new people.
- ◆ Voice your opinions in an environment you consider safe, at first; then experiment in more "daring" surroundings.

Strategies for Networking Most Effectively With Supportive People

- ◆ Ask for their opinions.
- ◆ Avoid confrontation.
- ◆ Avoid your impulse to interrupt their slower, deliberate responses or finish their sentences.
- ◆ Be patient in word and action.
- ◆ Be sincere.
- ◆ Break off the conversation amicably after a reasonable time; they will appreciate your effort.
- ◆ Don't push them into the spotlight.

◆ Draw them out by asking open-ended questions.

◆ Encourage them to venture forth and attend more events.

◆ Introduce them to your acquaintances.

◆ Invite them into a group and bring them up to speed.

◆ Offer to meet with them in their office or other familiar surroundings.

◆ Provide pleasant, warm surroundings with demeanor to match.

◆ Set parameters and clearly define goals.

◆ Show them that you are trustworthy by your actions.

◆ Slow down and let them catch up, if you are a Dauntless or Indefatigable style.

◆ Smile.

◆ Support their causes.

Example of a Supportive Networker

Judy takes a deep breath as she walks into the room that is already filled with other League of Women Voter members and guests. She deliberately stopped at the store on her way to the meeting, hoping she would be detained and have a legitimate reason for missing the networking hour.

Why were there no lines at the checkout counter? Why did traffic move so well? Here she is. She no longer has excuses.

Look at all these people! "Guest night" is always so much more frightening. It is harder to find people she knows. All of them seem surrounded by strangers.

Why did she even bother to come? A night at home with the family would have been so much more pleasant. Then she remembers the purpose of the group, the good it does for the community.

And, then, there is the opportunity to meet new clients.

She takes the plunge!

The Careful Networker

Again, Webster helps us out:

"... marked by wary caution or prudence, painstaking effort to avoid errors or omissions."

Careful networkers check the details before they attend an event or join a group.

- ◆ Can I get a list of attendees/members ahead of time?
- ◆ Does the event/group fulfill my marketing objectives?
- ◆ What do others say about the event/group?
- ◆ What is appropriate dress?
- ◆ What is expected of me?
- ◆ What is the format?
- ◆ Why is it being held?
- ◆ Why was I invited?
- ◆ Will it be worth my time and money?

Careful networkers are precise and analytical. Known for your deliberate approach to people and data, you do not like to make mistakes or be misquoted.

You are fastidious about your homework. Once there, you notice how people act in the parking lot, in the lobby, during registration. Rather than rushing into a roomful of strangers, you make a premeditated, conscious entry—always cognizant of people and happenings around you. Little escapes your observant eyes. You are an expert at evaluating, and you like to use data you collected about attendees before the event to help you immediately zero in on your targets. You continue to analyze during the conversation, always measuring what the other person says against your storehouse of knowledge.

Friends know your mind is like a computer, storing data that meshes with what is already programmed and tossing aside what doesn't fit. The wheels are constantly turning—assessing, keeping, tossing.

Small talk is not on your agenda. You prefer the meat and potatoes, allowing other styles to feast on salads and desserts.

Small talk is not on your agenda.

Your lack of spontaneity makes it hard for you to rebound when the people you have researched fail to show. You may feel at a loss, even frustrated, when you have to talk with others "blindly." You may consider the event ... and the organization ... a waste of time.

It can be beneficial to your relationship-building to ease up. Others may have difficulty living up to your high standards or may not choose to be in your network if you are so demanding. It's okay for you to choose perfectionism; however, it is not fair to expect others to do so, too.

Take an active role in planning networking events. Your eye for detail and your ability to organize are qualities others will value and benefit from. You can also learn and grow by working with others. It will help you overcome your desire to do everything yourself to make sure it is done "the right way."

You can benefit from a sign that says:

> **I am allowed one tiny mistake a day,**
>
> *and I seize the opportunity.*

Relationship-Building Strengths

- Accurate—shows up on time, on the right date and in the right place

- Analytical—researches events to ensure fit with marketing goals

- Careful—looks before leaping; scrutinizes people before beginning relationships

- Composed—is unruffled outwardly

- Conscientious—performs as promised and is reliable

- Observant—
  - Stores data for future reference
  - Watches carefully what is happening and reacts thereto

- Perceptive—reads body language well; therefore, is aware of what people are really communicating

- Persistent—doggedly pursues goals

- Precise—keeps track of even minute details

- Proper—
  - Knows etiquette and protocol and behaves and dresses accordingly
  - Prefers formality in appearance and demeanor

Relationship-Building Limitations

- ◆ Aloof—
  - Appears guarded most of the time
  - Behaves in a stoic manner
  - Exhibits sporadic eye contact
  - Shows little warmth and charisma
  - Speaks primarily with mouth, not with body
- ◆ Cautious—
  - Chooses words carefully and, sometimes, responds too slowly for fast-paced people who become leery of intent
  - Is wary of unknown people and circumstances
  - Misses opportunities because of uncertainties
  - Weighs pros and cons and cons and pros over and over
- ◆ Critical—criticizes self and others' performances
- ◆ Independent—prefers to do things alone, the "right way"
- ◆ Judgmental—judges others by own high standards, and lets others know when they "fail"
- ◆ Perfectionist—complains because few people, places or events meet high standards
- ◆ Restrained—appears uninterested and uncaring
- ◆ Sarcastic—appears caustic, with cutting wit

Suggestions for Improvement

- ◆ Accept minor inconveniences in physical surroundings.
- ◆ Accept others' shortcomings.

- Acknowledge your limitations.

- Increase self-confidence.

- Make quicker decisions/decrease research.

- Move outside comfort zone.

- Rely more on your intuitive abilities.

- Roll with the flow to increase other people's comfort level, also.

- Smile more.

- Tolerate ambiguity.

- Widen your space bubble to make others feel more comfortable.

Strategies for Networking More Effectively With Careful People

- Accept their lack of outward warmth and enthusiasm as normal.

- Be diplomatic even if asked the same question in various ways.

- Be logical; discuss pros and cons.

- Be organized so the value of speaking to you/attending the event are apparent.

- Be prepared; have your ducks in a row.

- Be specific.

- Become comfortable with pauses in the conversation; they need time to analyze data.

- Concentrate on their body language since they try hardest to conceal feelings.

- Don't ask personal questions.

- Don't take their nitpicking personally.

- Don't try to schmooze them.

- Explain precisely the nature of your business.

- Make them comfortable; usually they don't want to even be at the event.

- Take the lead to end the conversation diplomatically.

- Provide facts to back up your hypothesis. Explain precisely the nature of your business.

Example of a Careful Networker

Peter would rather be home reading the latest issue of Consumer Reports. *He's been shopping for a new car for six months and wants to read about the magazine's latest "best buys." He respects its thorough reviews and puts a lot of stock in its recommendations. After all, he used the same process to buy his last car, and he's been happy with it.*

However, he has researched his chamber of commerce's after-hours event tonight. The bank that is sponsoring it is on his list of potential customers, and he will have the opportunity to meet the president and other officers. Three of his other clients are attending and are bringing other decision makers from their offices.

The event only lasts for two hours. That means he can be home by 7:30 PM and still have time to read to the children, discuss the day with his wife and read the article by bedtime—if he leaves his briefcase in the office.

Oh well, it only happens once a month. Let's get on with it.

You've completed the initial step of learning your most comfortable networking style(s). Next, we'll examine two more key ingredients in your relationship-building process: (1) your personal image and printed image, and (2) the messages they continually send. To reinforce your knowledge of styles and help you integrate this information into your daily activities, we will refer to them throughout the book as you learn to increase your relationship-building savvy.

Part II

The Importance of Your
Personal Image
and Your
Printed Image

chapter 5

Impression Management

I n his famous soliloquy, Hamlet said:

"To be or not to be, that is the question."

I like to paraphrase those words to describe the ongoing 24-hour communication process:

To be is to communicate; there is no question.

You cannot *not* communicate. Communication affects every aspect of your life; therefore, it is essential to understand the process if you are to master relationship-building skills.

The success—or failure—of any interpersonal or written encounter begins the second a person lays eyes on you or picks up your printed materials. A professional image is key to starting the experience in the right vein. You never have a second opportunity to make that first good impression.

In this section, we will discuss the vital ingredients necessary to make—and keep making—a good impression through your personal image and your printed image.

Personal Image

People decide ten things about you within the first ten seconds of meeting you. According to William Thourlby, a contributor to the book *Image Impact*, they are:

1. Economic level

2. Educational level

3. Trustworthiness

4. Social position

5. Level of sophistication

6. Social heritage (your parents' and ancestors' social position)

7. Educational heritage (your parents' and ancestors' educational level)

8. Economic heritage (your parents' and ancestors' level of affluence)

9. Successfulness (in previous and current endeavors)

10. Moral character (6)

You may be thinking: "It's not fair. *I* certainly don't do that to others. You can't judge a cake by its icing. You need to cut a slice, examine the texture, take a bite, savor the taste— then voice your opinion."

In other words, you want people to meet you, talk with you, see your work—then decide about you. It would be nice if that were to happen.

It doesn't!

Animals use their physical reflexes to protect themselves in their natural habitats. They get set with every muscle ready to strike out at the perpetrator. Human beings also need to protect themselves in their personal and corporate habitats.

However, society does not allow you to physically strike your perpetrators and remain unfettered. Therefore, you use your mental reflexes to protect yourself in your personal and business surroundings.

Impression Management

You base your decisions about others on their image, which is a combination of their appearance and behavior: how they look and how they act.

Image = Appearance + Behavior

Since you are in charge of how you look and how you act, you are in charge of the impression you make on others and how you are judged. The art and science of creating and managing the impression you make on others is called *Impression Management*. Because you cannot exist without communicating, you are constantly making an impression on others.

The choice is yours: You can take charge and make it positive, or let it "happen" and deal with the consequences. It *will* happen.

After an expo for home-based businesses we both attended, Mike remarked to me that the first thing he had noticed in the parking lot on his way into the event was how casually people were dressed. Attired in a business suit, Mike asked me a rhetorical question: "Don't people realize they still need to project a professional look even when they work out of their homes?"

A female accountant in one of my communication courses remarked how she felt intimidated when male clients showed up at her home office in a dark suit and she was dressed in casual slacks and a blouse. She now wears a dark-colored skirted suit for first visits and continuing visits from certain clients and a dark blazer over slacks for others. She said the change in appearance has added to her confidence.

Jim, a massage therapist, works in casual clothes. On the evenings of his chamber of commerce's after-hours events, he changes into a suit. "It's important that people I meet perceive me as the professional I am. I know that my appearance plays a big part in it."

Let's take a closer look at the ingredients that comprise the appearance and behavioral sides of the image equation.

chapter 6

The Language
of Appearance

S ince your body is typically 90 percent clothed in business, what you wear plays a major part in how you are perceived. The other 10 percent is largely governed by your face so your hairstyle, beard or moustache, skin care and cosmetics also play a vital role, variously, for men and women.

Learn the One-Two-Three Punch!

On the appearance side, three key ingredients—color, style and fit—contribute toward making you a winner.

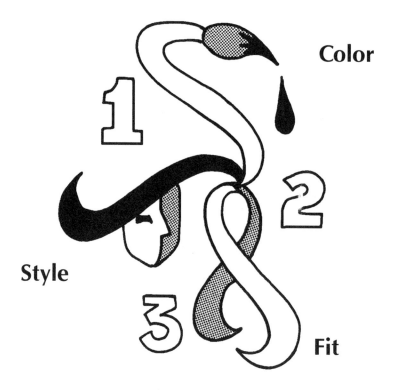

One: Color

Color affects people physically and psychologically. To convey your best image, be attuned to the effects of various colors and how to match them to each occasion or relationship-building opportunity. The right color varies with the event and sometimes aces out your favorite color when you want or need to create the right impression, mood or feeling.

Carlton Wagner, an internationally known expert on color, said:

> *"Remember, color is a language. It will speak for you. It always does the talking, whether you are conscious of it or not. Make certain that you are using color's wonderful ability to communicate to your advantage. Use colors to get the response you want. It will work for you!" (7)*

The positive and negative (in parentheses) connotations of different colors will guide you as you formulate your relationship-building plans. Analyze each situation to determine what impact you want color to have as part of your overall impression.

- **Black**—powerful, dignified, sophisticated, slimming (overwhelming, too powerful for some circumstances)
- **Blue**—calm, reliable, serene (lacking energy/excitement, "a case of the blues")
- **Blue-green**—dignified, prestigious, sophisticated (lacks mass appeal)
- **Brown**—dependable, practical, stable (weak, ordinary, lacks power/authority)
- **Gray**—successful, perception increases as shade deepens (gloomy, boring, uninteresting)
- **Green**—caring, friendly (unimportant, not serious)
- **Navy Blue**—authoritarian, knowledgeable, responsible (too powerful, all-knowing)
- **Orange**—accessible to the masses, informal (lacking class, inexpensive)
- **Pink**—friendly, flexible, sensitive (too soft, vulnerable)
- **Purple**—intuitive, regal, spiritual (unreachable, out-of-touch)
- **Red**—adventurous, dynamic, exciting (alarming, sexually arousing)
- **Yellow**—first hue the eye sees, sunny (transient, stress-inducing)
- **White**—clean, formal, sophisticated (detached, individualistic)

Two: Style

The second element encompasses both the style of the garments you choose, as well as your distinctive manner of putting outfits together. William Shakespeare gave us excellent advice about style that still is as relevant today as it was in the 17th century:

"Neither in the vanguard nor tail of fashion be."

Classic styles remain in vogue and project a middle-of-the road image, and, if you are on a budget, provide a much better value than the "latest fashion." Suits are still the accepted norm for men and women in most business environments, especially in corporate America. Some women who have "made it" tell me they feel free to dress more individualistically—dresses, skirts and blouses or slacks in any colors they choose.

I still "tote the line" for business. As Wagner points out, color creates a subliminal response. Pink will never connote the responsibility and knowledge that navy blue does. Because a jacket with long sleeves, slightly padded shoulders and a collar makes you appear one-third more powerful, a dress (especially if it is full of pastel flowers!) will never indicate the same professionalism as a suit. How can someone in a blouse or shirt sleeves change that innate perception?

**. . . a jacket with long sleeves, slightly padded shoulders
and a collar makes you appear
one-third more powerful. . .**

Your Distinctive Style—The look you create by the way you put together the different elements of your wardrobe—your style—speaks formidably. Here's where you can establish your individuality, within the framework of your preferences and your industry's guidelines. No two people accessorize exactly the same way. What you choose can either enhance or detract from your total look.

Your ensemble purveys considerable information to others about your attitude, confidence, organizational skills, self-esteem, self-respect and soundness of judgment. It is an outward map that guides others through your inner thoughts and actions; therefore, it can be a vital tool in relationship building and job seeking, or it can be an immense detriment.

Again, the choice is yours!

Three: Fit

You can select the right color, the correct style, the perfect accessories, but if they don't fit your body, you still are missing a piece of the puzzle.

You don't have to buy custom-made clothes. You have to ensure that your clothes *look* as if they were custom made. If you shop at a store that does not have a tailor, use your neighborhood tailor, who can accomplish miracles with a nip here and a tuck there.

**You don't have to buy custom-made clothes.
You have to ensure that your clothes look as if they were custom made.**

The money you spend to make the sleeves, pants and skirts the right length and the waistline fit yours will give you a polished look that increases your self-confidence and contributes to the positive aura you create.

Make sure the tailor measures both legs and arms since almost everyone's measurements vary from one side of the body to the other. Men, wear the shoes you will wear with the suit to make sure you get the correct pants length: a slight break on the top of the shoe. Women, wear the heels or flats you will wear with the outfit.

Additional Hints

◆ Accept the fact that you are getting older.

◆ Dress for the job you want, not the one you have.

◆ Emphasize quality, not quantity.

◆ Establish your professionalism, then experiment.

◆ Go for it—in your personal life.

◆ Individualize through your accessories.

◆ Look like a total package.

◆ Store your clothes with care and concern.

◆ Wear your best items on top.

For additional information on the appearance side of your image, refer to our workbook and audiotape, *Don't Wait Another 10 Seconds.*

chapter 7

What Body Language "Says"

B eing able to articulate well is important in relationship building. However, the effective use of the silent language, better known as *body language,* is even more crucial to your personal and professional success.

Body language has its own set of "grammar rules," and they include posture, gestures, facial expressions, eye contact and your use of space and time. Mastering body language, just as the spoken word, requires much more than memorizing theory. It takes knowledge plus desire, patience and skill.

Every face-to-face communication encounter has three elements: verbal, vocal and visual. Verbal (the words) contributes 7 percent. Vocal (tone, rate, pitch, inflection, rhythm) contributes another 38 percent. Visual (body language) is responsible for a whopping 55 percent. (8)

IMPACT

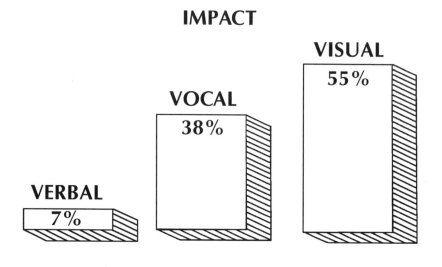

ABILITY TO CONTROL

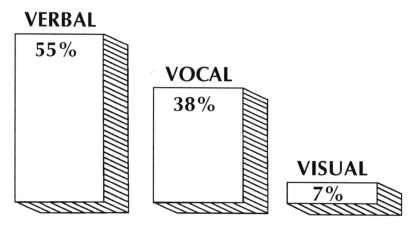

Elements of Face-to-Face Communications

Your ability to control the vocal part of your message is the same as its impact. Visually and verbally, the ability to control is inverse to its effect. Body language is difficult to manage for two reasons. First, it is subliminal. You unconsciously perform many actions. As you become more of an expert in nonverbal communication, you become more conscious of your own and others' unconscious movements.

Second, body language is an involuntary muscular reaction. Think of it this way: Have you ever tried not to sneeze when you have to? It's nearly impossible. You might stifle the sneeze, but eventually you still sneeze. Or, try consciously to keep your eyes open while you sneeze. That is virtually impossible. The same principle is true with body language. You might try to stifle some of the movements, but eventually, they "happen." That's why body language is so believable. It is natural, involuntary and cannot be easily manipulated.

Keep in mind that when you communicate on the telephone, you lose more than half the impact of the message because you cannot see the person. The vocal part of the message now constitutes 82 percent and your words 18 percent.

Posture and Handshakes

One of the first ways your behavior impacts relationship building is through your posture. You can walk into a room and, with the aura you create, command respect before you even say a word. Conversely, you can also lose respect without uttering even a "hello"! To gain respect, *you* need to know and respect who *you* are; others, then, will want to do the same.

To create a confident aura:

♦ Plant your feet.

♦ Hold your head high.

♦ Keep your shoulders back.

♦ Put your chest out.

♦ Hold your stomach in.

♦ Make eye contact.

Stand with your feet about six to eight inches apart, with one slightly in front of the other. This helps you feel balanced and grounded, which helps you feel more confident and in charge. It also allows you to easily shift weight from one foot to the other, which keeps you from "freezing in place."

To maintain good posture as you sit down, move your buttocks all the way to the back of the chair. If you scoot from the front to the back, you will bend your back along the way. Gone will be your erect posture, your confident aura and maybe even your edge in the conversation.

People also tell you through their posture whether they are approachable and want to include you in their conversation.

When two people are facing each other and forming a rectangle, they give the message they have "closed off" their space and do not wish to be interrupted. Most people do not consciously set out to do this, rather their bodies "close up the space" as they become more and more interested in the conversation. You set yourself for rejection when you choose to

try to join these two people ... and they are not yet ready to let you in. Sometimes, it can also be difficult for one of the people to break out when the other is not yet finished monopolizing the person.

> *I stopped by a funeral home to pay my regards to a friend when her father died. She had left for a little while so I met and spoke with her sister. We moved into a rectangle position, and I tried to break it as I needed to leave for an appointment. She kept following me to keep the box intact. It was apparent she was not yet ready to break off the conversation. Finally, a priest approached us, and as she saw him out of her peripheral vision, she opened our "box." I excused myself shortly after I was introduced to the priest.*

On the other hand, when two people have their feet pointed outward like two sides of an incomplete triangle, they are inviting you into the conversation.

Handshakes

Another vital element in the behavioral side of the image equation is a firm handshake. Many relationships have been aborted because a weak, spiritless handshake sent the same message about the person.

Men's handshakes are typically strong and firm because they naturally have a stronger grip. Women, if no one has has complimented you recently on your handshake, get a grip and beef it up—now!

Following are the ingredients of a good handshake:

◆ Hold person's hand firmly.

◆ Shake web to web.

◆ Pump hand three times maximum. (No milking strokes!)

◆ Maintain constant eye contact.

◆ Radiate positive aura.

Always wear your nametag on the right side. (At this point in my presentations, there is usually a whole lot of ripping going on!) People shake with their right hands even if they are left-handed. The tag on the right allows the eye to follow the hand and aids in registering your name in other people's minds.

Following are special types of handshakes to be cognizant of and / or avoid.

Controller—A person extends his hand to you, web-to-web, and as soon as your hands are linked, he purposely maneuvers his hand onto the top. There's no doubt that he is trying to take charge. While it may be impossible to undo the handshake, you will be a step ahead in the relationship when you make a mental note that the other person is trying to dominate.

Submissive—A person extends her hand to you palm up. She is telling you to take charge and be in control, that she does not feel worthy of meeting you on an equal basis. Your choices are to place your hand palm down and shake or to pull her hand side-by-side with yours.

Dead Fish—This is the slippery, damp palm someone extends to you—and you can't wait to remove your hand from his. If you are nervous and perspire in networking situations, carry a handkerchief or wipe your hands on your clothes. What you spend in cleaning bills will be paid for quickly in the better impression you make.

Limp Fingers—She extends only her fingertips, and you are not exactly sure how to grasp them or how hard to shake. Again, you will probably try to get out of this handshake as quickly as possible—if you got yourself into it in the first place. (One easy way to avoid this faux pas is to always extend your full hand vertically. Do not cup your fingers. Therefore, even if your handshake is limp, you give the other person something physically easier to grasp.)

Sandwich—Use this one only with people you know. When you envelop another person's hand like a vice, you're invading their private space (more on this in the next section). This may be used to show sincerity and concern *after* you know someone will appreciate it. It's also known as the politician's shake, which is enough to make most people avoid it!

Crusher—This one is practiced almost solely by men, and not always on purpose. It can be painful when done by a man with a big hand and strong grip on a woman with a smaller, more delicate hand. The pain is enhanced when a woman wears a ring on the right hand and the stone happens to be askew. (I always get nods from women who have experienced this.) If I know the man well, I'll pull away as I say, "Hey, I need to use this hand again." If I don't know him, I remove my hand as quickly as is feasible.

Limp Fish—Use your imagination. Put together the limp fingers and dead fish, and you get a handshake used mostly by women who have yet to learn the art of looking, acting and being powerful.

Refer to the next section for how far apart North Americans like to stand when shaking hands.

No Trespassing

The space around you—think of it as a bubble—is another important ingredient in your nonverbal communication. Each of you has a bubble, and the sizes vary. Rural people, for instance, normally have a larger bubble because they are used to wide open space. Urban people tend to have a smaller one because they live in more crowded conditions.

Your bubble has four different zones indicative of the "no trespassing" sign you wear in different situations. (9)

Knowledge of and understanding about people's zone preferences within their bubble can greatly enhance your relationship-building skills. Again, you must stay alert to people's actions and reactions to how you shake hands with them, how close you stand, etc.

Private Space

This area—about six to eight inches—is literally the space you regard as private. You want only people whom you have invited in to share this space with you. This is why the "sandwich handshake" offends many people. When someone uses her second hand to envelop yours, you may feel your privacy has been invaded. Some people extend their arm in its entirety to keep people from getting too close when shaking hands. Others even plant their elbows in their ribs when shaking hands to keep you from getting any closer.

If you are in the habit of patting people on the back or touching them on their arms or hands while talking, analyze the reactions you get. These gestures are taken by many as an invasion of their private zone. Going behind someone's desk without being invited is another example of "invasion."

Familiar Space

You reserve a space about 18 to 48 inches around you for people with whom you are familiar, but not necessarily intimate. It's the space where North Americans like to stand when shaking hands (typically about 24 -30 inches) and when talking with others.

In my workshops, I often ask participants to talk with another person, first at ten inches apart, then two to three feet apart. Try it—and you'll know why many people look relieved when they can back up!

People are less comfortable at networking events that are overcrowded and force them to stand closer than 18 inches from one another. You will find many people using a plate or a drink to act as a shield across their chests to guard their space.

When other people are too close, you become more aware of:

◆ Glasses/eye problems

◆ Height differences

◆ Inability to gesture

- Physical contact
- Skin imperfections
- Your breath
- Your voice intonations

Space invasion concerns also may arise when you talk with people from different cultures. Middle Easterners, Arabs and South Americans prefer to stand closer because they get much of their information through the senses of smell and touch. North Americans primarily get their information visually. They prefer to be farther back to get an overview.

When you find someone getting too close for your comfort, back up a step. If the person follows you, back up once more. After that, you may have to end the conversation as discreetly as possible, or tell the person of your discomfort. You don't want to end up backed into a corner with nowhere to go!

Social Space

Your social space ranges from 4 to 12 feet. This is where you stand at work when you stop by someone's office to visit or in your home with a repairperson. It's a nice, comfortable space to keep between you and someone you work with, know casually or may just have met in non-congested conditions.

Public Space

This space is reserved for circumstances you do not personally control or that do not demand close, personal involvement. It's the distance a presenter maintains between himself/herself and the audience, whether in the office or at a public meeting or conference. It begins at 12 feet and extends outward.

Generally, Careful and Supportive styles are most protective of their space. You may see them recoil or back up when they feel you are trespassing. Assertive, outgoing people are less restrictive of their space, with the Indefatigable style being the most touchy/feely.

What the Three Monkeys Tell Us

Those three monkeys—See No Evil, Hear No Evil and Speak No Evil—convey powerful messages in our relationship-building endeavors. In body language, these gestures are equated with human deceit: doubt, exaggeration, lying and uncertainty.

As a child, you put your hands over your eyes when you didn't want to see something, over your ears when you didn't want to hear something and over your mouth when you didn't want to speak.

As you grew older, you became more discreet with these gestures; however, you still use them with the same meaning. Instead of covering your eyes when you don't want to see something, doubt its truthfulness or don't want to face up to a situation, you rub your eye. When you don't want to hear what is being said, you may pull at your ear lobe or even put your finger inside your ear like a corkscrew. Instead of

covering your mouth, you may gently touch your lips or rub your nose when you doubt what is being said or think the truth is being stretched. Some disguise the hand-to-mouth gesture by faking a cough.

When people use these gestures while speaking, they may be purposely lying or exaggerating, or may not be confident of what they are saying. When listeners use these gestures, they doubt the veracity and accuracy of what is being said.

When you use hand-to-face gestures, you may inadvertently send negative messages, such as:

- ◆ "Don't listen to me."
- ◆ "I'm not sure what I am saying."
- ◆ "I'm lying."
- ◆ "I'm pulling your leg."

Bottom line: Touching your face while speaking weakens your relationship-building skills!

Arms

As you probably already know, when people's arms are folded, it indicates they are defensive, nervous, closed, angry, i.e., feel threatened. Your body movements mimic your attitudes. Someone who says folded arms feel comfortable is really telling you he/she is experiencing one or more of the above emotions. If you have a closed mind, you feel comfortable closing your arms. When you are really locked into an opinion, you will fold your arms and clench your upper arms with your hands.

Your heart is your most vulnerable area. Keeping it open to others shows you are open and accepting of them and their opinions. Shielding your heart conveys the opposite message.

The next time you become conscious of your folded arms, call "time out" and analyze what you are thinking or feeling. Don't be surprised if you are experiencing one or more of the emotions we just discussed. The person you are talking with, someone on television or the author you are reading has evoked it.

In networking situations, people exhibit negative or closed feelings by shielding their chests in several ways:

◆ Holding a drink / plate in front of them.

◆ Holding handouts, materials or a purse in front of them.

◆ Folding their arms.

◆ Holding one arm across chest or abdomen.

◆ Putting their hands in their pockets.

While people may consciously or unconsciously be trying to disguise their feelings, these feelings are genuine! Work at getting the other person's arms open as quickly as possible to affect an attitudinal change:

◆ Extend your hand if you have not yet shaken hands.

◆ Ask for a business card.

- Offer your business card.
- Suggest a visit to a display table or booth.
- Share a brochure or other materials.
- Suggest a visit to the buffet table.

If your attempts fail, you might be wise to take the partially closed arms as a signal to move on.

Facial Expressions

"He speakest not, yet there lies a conversation in his eyes."—Henry Wadsworth Longfellow

About 75 percent of your nonverbal communication is done with your face. It is essential to building relationships that you understand what your face and other people's faces are saying. Watch others' facial expressions to learn their emotions and gauge their feelings as you listen to their words. The same expressions can have vastly different meanings; therefore, it is vital that you "read" them in their immediate context.

- Down-turned eyes can connote guilt or shyness.
- A slight smile in the corner of the mouth can mean amusement or a mischievous thought.
- Raised eyebrows can mean surprise or incredulity.
- A jutted jaw can mean stubbornness or defiance.

Eye contact is an important aspect of relationship building. Let's "look" at how to use it effectively.

Where to Look

Imagine an inverted triangle in your face, the base of it just above your eyes. The other two sides emanate from it and come to a point between your nose and your lips. This is the

suggested area on which to focus your eyes for business conversations. (See illustration above.)

Socially, the point of the triangle drops to include the chin and neck areas. If someone's eyes travel to others parts of your body, it is probably more than business or a casual social situation they have in mind!

The triangles of good eye contact let you gaze in the vicinity of the face and ensure that you won't fixate on someone's eyes nonstop. Helpful hint: Look at one eye, then both, then one eye again.

Women generally need more practice in this area. They tend to look a man in the eye when he is talking but not when they are talking to him.

Historically, artists have painted lovers with the man looking at the woman, and the woman looking demurely down, reflecting what young girls were taught by their mothers years ago: "Don't come across too strong." "Don't be dominant."

Women, "demurely down" doesn't cut it in the business world! You must engage in direct eye contact to be taken seriously. If you have the opportunity in a meeting, stand up before you begin speaking, then look the audience in the eye and ask for what you want. Height is power, and it will add even more impact to your words.

How Long to Look

I suggest about 80 to 90 percent of the time. Anything less can be interpreted as evasiveness, discomfort, lack of confidence or boredom. To stare longer can be construed as being too direct, dominant or forceful and can make others uncomfortable. If you choose to establish your authority, stare longer. If you seek cooperation and equality, be less direct and stick to the 80 percent rule.

It's okay to glance down occasionally as long as your gaze comes right back up. Don't look away for any length of time. Others may construe it to mean you are lost in thought or looking for someone else to talk with.

When to Look

Begin the process as you start speaking with or listening to another person. Start it even earlier if you are trying to get another person's attention. Continue it throughout the conversation. Hold direct eye contact as you are saying good-bye—it leaves the other person with a strong, lasting, positive impression.

Smiling

Your smile is an important part of your facial communication. Again, the meanings run the gamut: concern, empathy, excitement, interest, love and condescension.

A "power" rule is to smile when you are pleased rather than to please.

Men are much better at the former; women tend to do the latter. Establish your presence in a room, *and then* smile. It is far more professional than to enter a room giggling or "all smiles." Use a smile to indicate that you would like to meet or speak with someone when your eyes meet. Use it also to show approval or agreement with what the other person is saying.

Nodding

Shaking your head can be used to show agreement or disagreement. Too much nodding will weaken you as a communicator. (Powerful people limit their gestures.) Also, nodding can encourage speakers to go on and on.

To get your turn in a communication exchange, stop nodding and assume a neutral expression. Generally, speakers will slow down and give you a chance to talk if they sense your interest is waning or that you have something urgent to say. If remaining expressionless doesn't bring an end to a conversation, interrupt—politely.

Study your facial expressions in a mirror or arrange to have yourself videotaped. Experiment to show different feelings. Become conscious of your various expressions so you can "see" what others are observing.

Mirroring

Copying another person's posture and gestures is a way to use body language to establish rapport in your networking activities. It lets other people know you approve of them and agree with them.

Mirroring can be done consciously in a business situation. David Lewis, author of *The Secret Language of Success*, has found that mirroring increases the chances of agreement by up to 50 percent during negotiations, and doubles your chances of making a favorable impression during sales presentations. (10)

> *My friend Janet Asbury, who illustrated this book, was intrigued with the "mirroring" concept from the moment I asked her to do the illustration for this segment. She decided to implement the theory in a sales*

call for her graphic design business in Orlando. When the client she was calling on crossed his legs, she did the same thing. When he picked up a pencil and gestured with it, she did so, too. Over and over, she diplomatically repeated his gestures and expressions. Bottom line? She called me soon thereafter and in her Indefatigable style said: "Incredible! It works, Lillian. It works! I practiced mirroring, and I got the job. The practice will be an integral part of my repertoire!"

Use mirroring to create a relaxed atmosphere when chatting with someone at a conference or meeting. Consciously mimic their facial expressions and body movements. For instance, if someone smiles, smile back. If they gesture with one hand, repeat the same gesture. Stand or sit the same way they are.

Use common sense! Don't overdo the process or make it look plastic. Also, if the person you are meeting with assumes a superiority position (hands behind head, and maybe even feet on the desk), don't mimic it. He/she will not find it complimentary if you do the same thing! Instead, be aware that the other person is trying to dominate, and be open and positive in your verbal, visual and vocal communication.

chapter 8

The Role of Seating Arrangements

Another way to create the illusion of power or equality in your relationship-building efforts is being cognizant of where you sit and where you seat others at meetings, conferences and after-hours events. Seating arrangements can help you better accomplish your goals.

Power Position

The power position in a meeting being held at a rectangular table is always in the center facing the door, where the person can see who is coming and going. On television clips, you'll notice it's where the president of the United States sits. The second most important position is to the person's right, the third to his/her left.

Cooperative

Let's assume in our illustration below that person A is calling the meeting. The most cooperative position is next to him/her (B) because there are no barriers between them. This position frequently is assumed in business and social situations by people who already know each other. While it is acceptable and recommended, this position rarely is assumed by business people meeting each other for the first time.

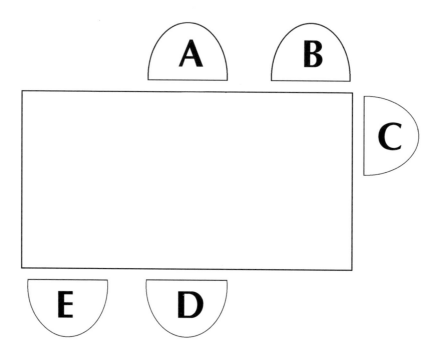

The next most cooperative position is C. Business people often use this arrangement at a first meeting or until they get better acquainted. It is recommended for a job interview. It allows two people to be close while still having the corner of the table as a safety zone.

Competitive

The most competitive position to A is D. The table is a barrier between them, and people may become competitive and defensive when seated across from each other. If you have a choice, like in a restaurant, sit in the corner position or ask for a booth. Don't set up a competitive situation unnecessarily. It can hamper an otherwise potentially positive relationship-building situation.

When seated in the competitive position, a person also becomes defensive about his/her personal territory (or half of the table). He/she may even push items into your half to make more room.

My husband and I went out for a casual dinner with another couple, and the four of us were seated across from each other, two and two. As soon as we sat down, the person directly across from me took the dessert list enclosed in a Lucite holder from her side and set it in "my half." She was protecting her territory. Rather than start a pushing match, I set it on a ledge next to our table!

Clients have been amazed by the frequent occurrence of the above behavior. It illustrates the importance of recognizing others' private space as discussed in "No Trespassing!" in Chapter 7. Pushing items into someone else's space is as much an invasion at dinner as if we had reached into their space and touched them.

A fourth position (E) is autonomous. It's across the table, and in the position next to competitive. It is where you sit when you need to share a table, and you do not want to be involved with the other person. You might choose it at a library or in a self-serve restaurant. You may have to share space, but not necessarily conversation.

Meetings

You can direct or control responses in a meeting through seating arrangements. Putting chairs in a circle demonstrates that you are encouraging equal contributions from all members. A horseshoe or "T" will recognize and emphasize people at the head of the table. Theater seating or side-by-side says, "You are here to listen, not to talk."

In a training situation, you can use circles for small group discussions, a horseshoe for workshops led by internal or external experts and theater seating for a keynote presentation. When you add a raised speaking platform, you are giving special status to the speaker, as well as setting up more of a barrier between him/her and the audience. Interaction is reduced; in fact, people usually wait to be called upon.

chapter 9

What Your Office and Your Car Say

While you may think only of your comfort and preferences when designing and furnishing your office, others may view it as an extension of your image, and, therefore, as another source of information about you. Your distinctive "lived-in look" provides visitors many clues about your relationship-building preferences, particularly if they are familiar with the networking styles we discussed earlier. Astute sales people will take it into account and might even modify their presentations once they see your office.

Because of your personal likes and dislikes, you will generally arrange your office similarly as you move from one job to the next, or when you strike out on your own. While budgets may restrict your opulence, you will still try to create your preferred effect, even if on a less grandiose scale.

Understanding what your own office environment says, as well as "reading" others' office environments, can put you a step ahead. As we discussed in Chapters 3 and 4, people like to deal and be dealt with in their natural behavioral styles. Knowing whether you can use your natural style, or if you need to modify it to get along better with the person you are calling on, can mean

- the difference between a pleasant experience or an unpleasant experience,
- closing the sale or letting it slip through your fingers, or
- the opportunity for a return visit if a sale is not eminent,

all of which impact your bottom line!

The following hints will help you discern people's behavioral style once you are inside their office. Even if employees are relegated to nearly identical corporate offices, you can still pick out their style through the individuality they express in their surroundings.

The Dauntless Office

- Huge power desk and chair—you stay behind it when shaking hands
- Overabundance of simultaneous activities:
  - E-mail—being received and sent
  - Employees "on call"
  - Fax machine—receiving or sending
  - People stopping by
  - Telephone ringing
- Overflowing out-baskets
- People in hallway being stopped as they pass by office
- Photos, if any, take second place to prominently displayed awards, plaques and trophies

Overall aura: authority, busy-ness, control, power

The Indefatigable Office

◆ Filing system: anywhere there's space, including floor

◆ Friendly, firm handshake from wherever you are; would prefer a hug

◆ Lots of photos of important people and not so important, as long as they include you

◆ Motivational posters and plaques

◆ "On alert" to entertain visitors *anytime*

◆ Several personalized or "special" coffee cups in use simultaneously

◆ Size of desk incidental, prefer to sit at table or on sofa to maintain closer contact

◆ Souvenirs to show where you have traveled

◆ Top of desk not visible since it was purchased

Overall aura: excitement, friendliness, fun, openness

The Supportive Office

◆ A place for everything, and everything in its place

◆ Cleared work space on desk

◆ Color-coded filing system

◆ Comfortable, conservative, subdued furnishings

◆ Everything in order

◆ Family photos and work "team" shots

◆ Neat piles of papers

◆ Plaques that recognize volunteer services

◆ Warm handshake from behind or in front of desk

Overall aura: calm, friendly, soothing, warm

The Careful Office

- ◆ Detached, formal handshake from behind desk
- ◆ Diplomas, charts, graphs on wall
- ◆ Few photos, seldom family-related
- ◆ Furniture arranged for functionality, not for visitors, who may be considered an interruption to orderly flow of day
- ◆ State-of-the-art technology
- ◆ Visible desk top, few adornments or papers
- ◆ Well-coordinated decor

Overall aura: efficiency, formality, functionality, orderliness

Vehicles

Your automobile is another extension of your image, and, as such, is just as important in making that good first and ongoing impression. Pretend each day that you will be driving your most important client or customer to lunch. Then, if it happens unexpectedly, you will be prepared.

Some companies have a policy of sending an employee to check out your car in the parking lot while you are being interviewed for a job.

Among the impressions your vehicle may create are:

- ◆ "It looked like a fast-food restaurant container repository."
- ◆ "Was that Sunday's paper in the back seat? Or maybe it was the entire week's worth—the pile was so large!"
- ◆ "Evidently, he has his shirts done at the cleaners, and he takes them every two weeks."
- ◆ "Is that crumpled towel covering a hole in the seat, or did she take her dog to the vet?"

Cars, like clothes and other elements of your living and work environments, tell others about your cleanliness, organizational abilities, self-respect and sound judgment.

And, yes, they even "talk" about your preferred styles. Dauntless people like full-size luxury cars like Mercedes Benz, BMWs and Cadillacs. Indefatigable types like sleek sports cars, often red ones. Supportive people are content with practical vehicles like standard vans in conservative browns and blues. Careful styles? Check the latest issue of *Consumer Reports* for their top pick ... you can be sure it is functional.

An equally high Dauntless and Indefatigable style may have trouble choosing between a BMW and a Corvette. Maybe, one of each is the answer!

chapter 10

Your Printed Image

A polished, professional printed image needs to precede your grammatically correct, succinct message. People see the vehicle you use to convey your message—before they read it. They look at and touch (and yes, even feel!) your business card, your stationery, your brochures and handouts before they read them.

These pieces are marketing and support tools for sales and customer service. They establish, build and maintain relationships with your customers and the public. To people you have not yet met or who may never meet you personally, your literature *is* the company. Your printed materials convey your spirit, your image—it's your corporate personality! For people who know you, it is a continuation of your professional image.

Your printed image is your corporate personality.

Top corporate executives ranked printed materials second only to annual sales figures in judging the positive image of a company, according to a study done in the 1990s by Yankelovich, Skelly and White/Clancy and Schulman, Inc. The nationwide corporate identity study of a hypothetical company showed 92 percent of the executives stressed factors such as professionalism and readability as key.

The initial image people consciously and subconsciously make about your materials is based primarily on the following elements:

- Color
- Design
- Stock (paper)

I believe in doing well what you do and hiring others to do what they do well. While computers and software packages can make desktop publishers out of almost anybody, there's still real merit in hiring a graphic designer to help you project a professional image to your clients and prospects. A professional image provides the edge entrepreneurs need to get in the door, to make up for the experience and customers their companies do not yet have. Once established, the business must maintain and preserve that professional appearance to keep its marketing and sales edge.

Large corporations spend millions of dollars on logo design. You need to likewise invest the time and dollars necessary (on a much smaller scale!) to develop a logo and printed materials that convey the image and message you want.

Talk to business associates, friends and family about your business and what image you want the materials to conjure up. Test several designs *before* you make a final decision.

Ultimately, you need to make the final decision! It is *your* image, and you need to feel good about it.

Case Study

When creating Duoforce Enterprises, Inc., I started with the name itself. I wanted it to be powerful, to make an impact, to be a force to be reckoned with.

The "force" part came easily. The challenge was what to combine with it. My husband and I brainstormed for days, with the dictionary and thesaurus close by.

"Duo" became the right fit. It shows

◆ personal and professional development,

◆ the client and me, and

◆ inner and outer growth.

I explained our rationale to the designer, who took our thoughts and turned them into art. The slant of the "force" shows the power and forward movement I wanted. The outline of the "Duo" shows the openness of the company and provides warmth.

I chose a 70-lb. ivory stock for the stationery: ivory meaning clean, formal, sophisticated. The ink is teal: prestigious, sophisticated—and it appeals equally to men and women.

For a unified look, the designer prepared artwork for stationery, a second sheet with just the logo, envelopes, a foldover business card, invoices and labels. My website, www.duoforce.com, also features a teal and ivory look.

Further, I found a tabletop exhibit in teal and complement it with a velvet teal cloth that gives it a much richer look than the ordinary table cover at a tradeshow.

In Chapter 13, we take an in-depth look at how to use business cards because they are vital marketing tools. Here, we examine color, design and stock applicable to all your printed pieces.

Color

The following hints will help you choose a color(s) for your company:

◆ Refer to the information in Chapter 6 to assist you in choosing the right color for the image you want to project.

◆ Reflect on your personal likes/dislikes. No matter how right a color might be for others, if you don't like it, don't use it!

◆ Achieve a two-color affect by using a colored ink for your logo and a colored stock.

◆ Consult with your graphic designer or printer.

◆ Test market with people whose opinion you value.

Design

◆ Decide what image you want your company to convey.

◆ Do you need serif or sans serif type to get your desired effect?

◆ Do you want an icon (symbol) or type alone?

◆ Interview several designers; ask to see samples of their work.

◆ Test market sample designs (most designers will give you several to choose from) with associates before you go to final art.

Stock

- ◆ 20-lb. paper is the weight generally used for copying, faxing, etc.

- ◆ 24/60-lb. paper is a better quality and works well for fliers and handouts. It usually does not bleed through (contents of one side can't be seen on the other).

- ◆ 70-lb. paper is the general choice for stationery. It adds an even more professional look to fliers.

- ◆ 67/80-lb. cover stock is the usual choice for business cards. It will not bend with normal handling. As with stationery stock, there are myriad colors, textures and designs to choose from.

- ◆ Check with your designer/printer for your particular needs.

We've introduced you to your networking style and helped you understand how your personal image and printed image affect your relationship-building success. Now, we are ready to take an in-depth look at the many practices and techniques that contribute to your networking success.

Part III

The Art
and Science
of Networking

chapter 11

Goal Setting

The first step in achieving all you can from your networking endeavors is to know what you want to accomplish. It's time to set goals—in writing! Then, you need to set time lines and allocate money and other resources so you carry out your networking activities in a planned fashion and meet your objectives.

As you reach your goals or even make progress toward reaching them, reward yourself! Take time to enjoy and feel good about each step along the way; you have accomplished something. Your self-esteem increases when you accomplish your goals. Get in the habit of rewarding yourself. Higher self-esteem makes it easier to reach your next goal, which makes you feel even better about yourself! You are in the winner's circle.

Take whatever time is necessary to answer all the questions in this chapter. This information will set a solid foundation or reinforce your existing base for relationship-building activities.

What Is the Focus of Your Business/Career?

This is the first question you need to answer because it will establish or refine your direction. If you are self-employed, this information can come from your business or marketing plan. If you have neither of these, back up and prepare them before you go any further. If you work for someone else, use your one-year, five-year or ten-year career plan as your basis.

Who Are Your Potential Clients/Employers?

The following Master Relationship-Building Plan is designed for you to use in your goal-setting process. Begin by making an exhaustive list of whom you want to meet, again gearing it to clients/customers or potential employers. If you want to be promoted or move laterally, prepare a list of who can be instrumental in moving you along your path. Include people in your company and your industry as well as influential people in other companies and industries.

Let your mind go! Remove any barriers. At this point, anyone you want to do business with or work for is a candidate for your list.

Fill as many pages as you can. Keep your plan current. Check back to see who is important, who used to be important. Why are/aren't these people in your current plan? Who needs to be added? Why?

At this time, complete only the "who" column.

Master Relationship-Building Plan Chart

Potential clients or employers	Where to meet them	Where to meet people who know people I want to meet	Whom I already know who knows them	Status: H = hot L = lukewarm C = cold D = defunct

Date_____ 1st Revision_____ 2nd Revision_____

Permission to reproduce is given by Duoforce Enterprises, Inc.

Where Can You Meet Them?

This step helps you zero in on appropriate organizations and clubs to join. Many people skip this step and join groups based on instinct or the "high" of a first meeting. People frequently share with me how much money they have spent on "joining" organizations—with no measurable return. (This is especially painful when you are self-employed and the dues/entertainment costs come out of your pocket!)

How Do You Find Groups to Join?

Begin by scanning this generic listing:

- Chambers of commerce
- Civic
- College alumni
- Education
- Fraternity alumni
- Industry
- Networking
- Philanthropic
- Professional
- Religious
- Social

Then get more specific, adapting the following suggestions to meet your needs.

1. Ask your local chambers of commerce for a list of organizations (and even surrounding chambers if you live in a densely populated suburban area surrounding a major metropolitan area like Chicago). Almost all of them have a comprehensive, annually updated list of all professional, civic and social groups that meet in their town/area.

2. Attend local chamber events to determine if membership might be advantageous. The Naperville Area Chamber of Commerce, to which I have belonged for more than 10 years, is one of the largest in Illinois with more than 2,000 members. In addition to the standard before- and after-hours events and luncheon meetings, it also sponsors a variety of committees. A targeted one is the Trainers and Consultants Connection, which I headed for a year. It has led to numerous income-producing alliances with peers. I also helped start a chamber speakers bureau and that, too, has led to paid speaking and training programs that started by my donating a one-hour program locally.

3. Check with the national office of an organization you may have belonged to in college or another city to find local chapters. For instance, my social sorority, Alpha Chi Omega, has many active alumnae groups in the Chicago area.

4. Join a focused business leads organization if you have a product or service to sell. These run the gamut from being part of international organizations to those that have only one chapter started by someone locally. They tend to be category-exclusive and are an excellent place to hone your networking skills and peddle your wares in a comfortable peer environment.

5. Clip the calendar listings from local newspaper(s) for a month to get a feel for the types of groups that meet in your area. A contact name and/or number are always included.

6. Ask people ... like your neighbors; co-workers; school, church and synagogue acquaintances; bankers; and insurance agents what they would recommend.

   When I moved to Downers Grove IL, where I knew no one, from Kalamazoo MI, where I had been so active at work and in the community, I talked to my insurance agent, who was one of the first people to call on me. He said the owners of the local paper were his friends, and I could use his name to introduce myself and let them know I had a journalism degree from the University of Missouri. I did just that. While I never spoke to them about a job, we did become friends, and they were great supporters for more than 25 years and generous in the editorial space they allocated to my endeavors.

7. If you are moving to a new city, ask people in your current community whom they might know in the area to which you are relocating.

   On a personal note: I was pregnant with my second son when we moved to Downers Grove. I asked my doctor if he could refer me to an obstetrician in that general area. Granted, it was a long shot, what with six million people in the Chicago area. Turns out one of his medical school friends had a practice less than 10 miles from my new home. Since then, I have moved and now am only five miles from the office! You never know if you don't ask.

8. Start your own group. That how I became the president of Better Business Contacts, a business leads group that I owned in the Chicago area for 10 years.

Once you have narrowed your choices, visit the group, and answer the following questions:

- ◆ Are the dues/meal costs affordable?
- ◆ Did you agree with the ideology?
- ◆ Did you feel comfortable?
- ◆ Did you like the mix of people?
- ◆ Did you thoroughly understand the purpose?

- ◆ Is the meeting time convenient?

- ◆ Were members interested in meeting you?

- ◆ What percent of the members attend functions?

Now, return to your master plan and list specific organizations in the second column.

Get Involved

Once you have decided to join an organization(s), get involved! Volunteer to serve on a committee, agree to head a project or join the ambassadors or welcoming committee so you have a legitimate reason to greet people as they arrive. Eventually, agree to head the committee or to serve on the board of directors, if asked.

Just attending monthly meetings will not help you reach your goals. Getting to know people better in small work groups will. It's also better to get actively involved in one group than to participate minimally in several.

Being involved in organizations also can help sharpen your presentation skills. Speaking in front of others is the number-one fear of Americans. (11) Become comfortable speaking in front of a small, friendly group. Then, transfer that comfort level and confidence to other groups.

To be successful in selling yourself, your products or services, you need to learn to speak to people and in front of people. Your printed materials will help communicate your message; you can also hire telemarketers. Eventually, though, as former President Harry Truman said: "The buck stops here."

You may choose to be coached in the skill or to refer to our workbook or audiotape, *Speak Easy: Overcome the Number One Fear*, to further allay your fears.

Where Can You Meet People Who Can Introduce You to Your Target Market?

Another benefit of joining organizations is to meet people who can introduce you to potential clients/customers/employers. Use the same procedure previously outlined to help you zero in on this target audience. Then, list your target groups in the third column of your master plan.

Now, complete the final two columns in your relationship-building plan. The fourth column asks whom you already know who knows your potential clients or employers. (I do not espouse including people with whom you have not bothered to stay in touch.) Column five asks for the status. Use a pencil to complete this area so you can update it regularly. Our key explains that H = hot; L = lukewarm; C = cold; D = defunct.

What Do You Want to Achieve Through Networking: Short-Term/Future?

What specifically do you want to accomplish?

A short-term goal may be to join your local chamber of commerce. A long-term goal may be to get three new clients annually through your membership. Steps to reach these goals might be:

1. Join the chamber.

2. Attend monthly luncheons.

3. Attend before- and after-hour networking events.

4. Join the ambassador committee.

5. Chair the ambassador committee.

6. Serve on the board of directors.

Each step will get you more intimately involved with the organization and acquaint you with an increasingly larger number of influential members.

List your short-term and long-term networking goals.

How Much Time and Money Can You Afford to Spend on Networking?

Be specific in your answers to these two important issues. Time is a valuable commodity; yet, you cannot afford not to spend time building relationships since they are invaluable to your future. Consider that:

◆ Warm calls (those backed by a referral from someone else) produce 80 percent more results than cold calls.

◆ At least 85 percent of all jobs are found through referrals.

Time

Be practical about the time you can afford. Look at your calendar for the upcoming month. Check the previous few months. How much spare time do (did) you have? How much time have you spent attending meetings/events? What business can you attribute to the group? Continue to track your business sources. It takes time to build solid relationships!

Money

How much can you afford to spend on networking? How much can you afford not to spend? Can you take a client to breakfast instead of dinner and have money left to pay for a luncheon meeting? Are there any low-cost or free activities sponsored by local colleges, community groups and corporations at expos or conferences? Decide now how much time and money you will allocate for networking activities for the next 6 to 12 months. Review your numbers monthly or quarterly.

Be Realistic

Rome wasn't built in a day; neither is a strong, solid network. It takes time; it takes work; and it takes savvy. At some events, you add bricks to your foundation; at others, you add only a tablespoon of mortar. Yet, all are necessary to the completion of your house of contacts.

Some people call it luck—being in the right place at the right time. Goal setting helps make you lucky. It gets you to the right place to meet the right people. It will just "happen" once you have determined and refined your goals. The more directed your goals, the more directed your efforts will be— the more quickly you will get your business started, grow your existing company, move laterally or find a new job.

Give your subconscious mind direction, and it *will* lead you to people and events that will bring you closer to your goals.

chapter 12

Your Verbal Business Card

Once you have set your goals, there are two key things you must have ready at all times: your verbal and printed business cards. In this chapter, we'll look at those all-important introductory words that describe what you do— words that will capture others' attention and hold their interest. Your first words last forever!

Your first words last forever!

Your appearance and behavior may already have made a positive impression—now, your words must maintain or accelerate the interest others have shown in you. Don't lose even a few seconds at this crucial time. No "ahs" or "ums" allowed here. You are the expert on you!

I've developed a process that will help you develop the two or three sentences that succinctly tell others what you do. It's important to note that this is not what people commonly refer to as your *elevator speech*, which may be between 30 and 60 seconds. This one lasts only about 10-15 seconds because that's all the time you have to grab someone's initial attention ... and that's all the time it is proper for you to use before giving the other person a chance to speak.

It's wise to develop several verbal business cards, one for use at community, civic and professional organizations; one for internal use; and one for your industry. At the latter two, jargon is acceptable and even expected. At the first one, it is verboten.

Branding

We begin the process by helping you establish your brand, which is who you are. Your image, by the way, calls your brand to mind, so it is helpful to make them mutually supportive. You already have a brand and an image, whether you have consciously worked on them or not.

Your imaging includes your appearance, behavior, brochures, resumés and business cards. We have already discussed many of these items in depth elsewhere in the book.

Now, it's time to look more closely at how to establish a positive brand. Let's start the process by answering four key questions that are relevant whether you are self-employed or work for someone else.

What Do You Do?

To help you answer this simple, yet thought-provoking question, I've come up with more questions to stimulate your thinking.

- What services do you provide?

- Who's your target market?

- What tasks do you perform?

- What do you say when people ask *you* the question?

How Do You Do It Differently?

Here's where your uniqueness begins to shine through. Again, a few more questions:

- What makes you different from others who provide the same service?

- What value do you add?

Suggestions to get you thinking: Do you walk your talk? Are you a good listener? Are you a published author? Are you the top producer in the company? Have you experienced what you sell, speak about or teach?

How Do You Deliver Your Services/Products?

- What methods do you use?

- What vehicles do you employ?

How Do You Do It Differently?

- What value do you add in your delivery?

- Why would people hire you vs. someone else who provides a similar service?

- What makes your presentation, delivery and customer service stand out?

To help you formulate your answers, ask others why they purchase your services or products. You may discover a uniqueness you don't even tout! In any case, you are sure to get useful information.

Turn Your Features Into Benefits

Just as good advertising copy always includes benefits—so must your introduction. People buy a stove primarily because it cooks food, not because of its height or color. Why do people buy your products and service? What benefits do they receive by dealing with you? What you need to do is turn your/your company features into benefits. Keep in mind that features are characteristics and highlights. Benefits are advantages and outcomes.

That I have owned my own business for more than 10 years is a feature. That I have worked with entrepreneurs and Fortune 100 companies during that time and how I use the experiences to help you is a benefit. The fact that I use Inscape Publishing assessment tools is a feature. That I have extensive, award-winning experience with DISC and can apply it to almost any business or personal situation that arises is a benefit.

This is a simple process, not necessarily an easy one. Be willing to spent time on it! Again, ask clients and peers how they benefit from working with you. Ask your boss what he/she values as your greatest contributions.

Every time you plan a sales call, take time to turn your features into benefits for the potential/actual customer. You will find it well worth the time and effort!

**Every time you plan a sales call,
take time to turn your features into benefits
for the potential/actual customer.**

Verbal Business Card Ingredients

Here are content suggestions for a general introduction. You can vary as you see fit for your internal and industry ones.

To Be Included

Your first and last name is vital even if you are wearing a nametag (more on introductions in Chapter 15). Also vital is *what you do.* Ever notice how many people tell you who they are and how they do what they do ... rather than what they do, which is what you asked? Include the benefits you have derived from your features. Lastly, use active verbs. Verbs are considered active when the subject performs the action ... exactly the feeling you want to convey. They add zest and vitality to your speaking even when you naturally are not a zestful and vital speaker. Take advantage of them!

Probably Not Included

Do not include your company name unless it adds value to your first few seconds of interaction. When I worked for AT&T in the 1980s, I often used the company name because of the positive connotation. I don't use Duoforce Enterprises, even though I am proud of my company. It is not a household name and, therefore, doesn't add immediate value.

Leave out your company location unless for some reason it will intrigue or interest someone else. (It can be vital for internal interactions when you work for a company with multiple locations.)

My grammar lesson here is to avoid adjectives and adverbs. They reflect opinions, usually yours, and often are exaggerated and superfluous. Refrain from telling people you are the best, quickest, greatest or most reliable within the opening seconds of meeting them.

Not Included

This is not a time to flaunt titles like CEO, COO, president, vice president or company founder. Titles may make it appear as if you need to affirm your self-worth. Also shy away from business labels like accountant, attorney and trainer. Again, they add little value in those precious first moments. For instance, if I were to introduce myself as a trainer, it could be interpreted in many ways such as an animal trainer, personal trainer, soft skills trainer, technology skills trainer, etc. You want to keep people's mind on you, rather than giving them a reason to ponder what kind of trainer you are.

Avoid "how" you do it at this point. Again, I might deliver my services through training … but I'm not yet ready to get into that. I want to intrigue them with the "what."

Also, stay away from exaggerated claims (easier to do when you eliminate adjectives and adverbs) and industry jargon.

Here are some before and after examples from people I have coached in the process:

> *Before: I'm John Smith (name has been changed), and I'm a psychologist. I do stress management programs to help you get over the stress in your career, especially when you lose your job.*

> *After: I'm John Smith, and I have developed a three-point program to help you take your career to a new level.*

John had come to me concerned that people were not being receptive to his introduction. In his case, particularly, his business label of psychologist was not a plus. The last thing people in transition want to hear is that they might need a psychologist to help them!

Before: I'm Ron Jodlowski, and I provide turnaround and operations benchmarking in areas of quality, cost, supplier performance, productivity and other critical points of performance for a healthier business.

After: I'm Ron Jodlowski. I help start-ups through mid-sized companies prosper and grow. I locate and solve problems in areas such as financial, personnel, operations, sales and marketing.

I've had many iterations of my own verbal business card over the years. My current one is:

I'm Lillian Bjorseth. I make it easier for entrepreneurs through Fortune 100 employees to meet people and get along with others by improving your networking and communication skills. I also help you polish your presence and make polished presentations.

And, I vary it with the occasion. Often, I will say,

"I help you increase your comfort level with meeting and getting along with others."

I find that the first example is most useful when introducing myself to a group of people because it conveys in a subtle way that I coach, train and speak, i.e., I work with individuals and companies.

Your Verbal Business Card

Based on all you have read, it's now time for your to create your card. Use this format. I am (your first and last name), and I (help, work with, share) and the rest of what you do.

Use simple, short words that people can understand immediately. They may still be looking at your appearance or posture or trying to catch another glimpse of your nametag and are not capable of digesting unfamiliar words (like Duoforce Enterprises) simultaneously. Your goal is to be understood. When creating your message, keep in mind the five Ss:

- ◆ Sensible

- ◆ Sincere

- ◆ Special

- ◆ Stimulating

- ◆ Succinct

Rehearse the words until they flow easily and naturally. Try them out on your family, friends and associates. Ask for their input. Accept constructive criticism. Fine-tune the words until you are ready to try them out on strangers. Revise and improve if you don't get your desired results.

The "How"

One of the ways to test if your verbal business card is working is to make sure it invokes the one question you want asked, "How do you do it?" Then you can launch into what most of you have been eager to share. We are always much better prepared to answer *how* we do it. Here are some examples:

> *John Smith: As a coach and workshop presenter, I help people who are employed and those in transition reach new levels in their career. I've developed customized approaches to assist people reach their goals.*

Ron Jodlowski: As a senior business advisor, I help companies grow by benchmarking key performance indicators. I also provide interim leadership and senior and key management training.

Lillian Bjorseth: I help people grow personally and professionally through personal coaching and as a relationship-building consultant, trainer, speaker and author. (The latter usually invokes the question, "What have you written?" This provides another good conversation entrée for me.)

This is an example from someone who needs coaching!

"I'm (name withheld) with (name withheld) and we have the second largest collection of xxxx." My first question of him was not, "How?" rather, "Why do you give your competition air time in the first words of your introduction?" Three times he said to me, "You have a valid point. I never thought of it like that." I trust he does now!

Top-of-the-Mind Positioning

Another benefit that comes from the process I have created is that it also helps you focus on your top-of-the-mind positioning. This simply means that people think of you first / refer you first when they or someone they know needs your products or services. Yours is the first name that comes to mind.

Now that you have created your verbal business card and have carefully thought through what you do differently and how you provide it differently, it will be easy for you to list the products and services you want people to associate with you. Be liberal and list all of them.

Next, choose the one or two you want people to associate most with you and write on a separate piece of paper:

When people think of (product/service), they think of
(your first and last name.)

Example: When people think of networking, they think
of Lillian Bjorseth.

Now put this information where you can see it daily and let it guide you in your branding/imaging efforts!

The last step is to deliver your verbal business card with class and confidence. Refer to Chapters 6 and 7 for refresher tips. Convey confidently that you know who are and what you do!

Now let's examine in depth the second key element that needs to be omni-present in relationship building.

chapter 13

Why Business Cards Are Invaluable

Printed business cards, next on your agenda after completing your verbal business card, should be prepared immediately upon starting a business (preferably, as soon as you choose a company name and address and before you are even "in business"). The same holds true if you are between jobs—obtain simple black and white cards as quickly as possible. Business cards are your most effective, least expensive form of advertising. At a nickel or dime apiece, this 2-inch by 3 1/2-inch piece of paper has the potential to generate millions of dollars of revenue.

There is no excuse (and I have heard lots of them!) for not having this invaluable tool with you at all times. Distribute your business card whenever and wherever feasible. Consider it your calling card to your dreams!

**Consider it [your business card]
your calling card to your dreams!**

Let's examine the contents of the card before we discuss how to use it.

Get Your Nickel's or Dime's Worth

Compare your cards to others. See how your business card stacks up to these important guidelines:

◆ Attractive and pleasing to the eye

◆ Easily read and understood at a glance

◆ Appropriate use of company colors and logo

◆ Inclusion of name, title, company, phone and fax numbers, and e-mail and web addresses

◆ Additional information if your company name is not descriptive

Because Duoforce Enterprises does not describe my business, I use a fold-over card with the top half ending one-quarter inch from the bottom of the card. Duoforce Enterprises, Inc., as well as my name and title, are printed on the top half. On the bottom one-quarter inch are the words, "Author. Consultant. Speaker. Trainer." When you open the card, the top half contains:

Our promise:
To make it easier for you to meet people and target your market
improve communication within and outside the organization
polish your presence and make polished presentations
... to increase individual and business success!

The lower half contains my name and title again as well as address, phone and fax numbers, and e-mail and web addresses. The back of the card lists all my published products and that I am an authorized Inscape Publishing Inc. distributor.

You may choose to have your business card perform multiple marketing functions by including information on the back even when it is not a fold-over card.

Following are some examples of good "back side" uses:

◆ A medical doctor who encourages patients to remember their appointments by listing the days of the week with a blank line (on which to write the date) under each on the back of his card.

◆ A motivational speaker who has an inspirational message printed there.

◆ An insurance agent who uses it to print a 12-month calendar (on slick paper).

◆ A health club that uses it as an invitation for a free visit.

◆ A cosmetics company that uses it to promote free facials and a business opportunity with the company.

◆ A golfing supply store that uses it to list the brands it carries.

◆ A chiropractor who uses it for a map to her office.

◆ A mortgage lender who uses it to tell customers what they need to bring to a loan application meeting.

◆ An industrial cleaning company that describes ideal "jobs."

The front of your card also can become an enhanced marketing tool—particularly if you are in the creative arts.

◆ A photographer friend uses a variety of his stunning photos as four-color business cards. Type is kept to a minimum: his company name, phone number, e-mail and web addresses.

♦ An exhibit company uses a parchment card, which shows their good taste and creativity.

Color photos individualize cards and help identify the giver. They've become a standard among Realtors and many professional speakers.

Stick with the standard 2-inch by 3 1/2-inch size or one that folds to that size. Business card cases, vinyl holders and trays accommodate them. The cylinder desktop card holders are passé. I still occasionally get one of those fancy die-cut cards and cringe at how much money the owner wasted as I cut it "down to size." People who store their information on computers or hand-held electronic devices still "handle" your card at events and need it to make sure they get all the vital statistics.

Look at your card again—carefully. Would *you* know what your company does if you were looking at it for the first time? If there is any doubt, have it redone now! Get your nickel or dime's worth!

Let's move on to a multitude of tips to help you use your well-designed card properly and effectively.

Be Prepared

Always carry your business cards! This is the easiest, greatest revenue-generating tip to implement; yet, it is often abused. It continues to amaze me how many people want to build relationships and yet are "cardless" at the most inopportune times. Running out of business cards or forgetting them makes an impression—an unfavorable one that screams lack of preparation and organization.

Running out of business cards or forgetting them makes an impression— an unfavorable one that screams lack of preparation and organization.

The following are some of the most-heard, and amusing, excuses:

◆ "They are in here somewhere," she says, rummaging in her handbag.

◆ "I haven't really started my business yet."

◆ "I didn't know I would be coming here tonight."

◆ "They are in my briefcase." (Nowhere to be seen!)

◆ "Honey, I'll give you my *home* phone number." (I don't want your home number, dear!)

◆ "I have on a different suit today." (Good!) "They must be in my other jacket."

◆ "They are at the printers."

◆ "I am in transition." (Have some printed immediately with your name, address, phone number and area of expertise.)

◆ "I only brought a few, and I want to give them to prospective clients." (Actual comment from a fellow speaker/trainer. For some reason, I have lost my interest in referring her!)

◆ "They must be in the handbag I used yesterday."

◆ "I had two other meetings today, and I ran out."

◆ "I always carry them with me on business." (Overheard at a Saturday morning meeting—What is this event?)

◆ "They must be in my car."

◆ "My boss doesn't think I need them."

◆ "I must have misplaced them."

◆ "I had no idea I would go through so many so fast. I'll drop one in the mail." (I have yet to get one of those!)

◆ "Didn't I already give you one?"

- "I ran out of the office/house in such a hurry I forgot them."

- "Let me check. No, these aren't mine. Must have given my last one away."

- "I spilled my drink on them."

- "I don't have any yet."

- "The girl who orders them is on vacation, and the rest of us don't know how to do it." (Too bad, boys!)

- "We're still deciding on a name for our company."

- "Never carry 'em."

- "I left them in my desk."

- "I only work part time."

- "They've been on order for two weeks. You know how it is when you depend on other people."

- "I left them in my hotel room."

- "We haven't agreed on our logo yet."

- "We've had so many other start-up expenses."

- "We are waiting until we move to a permanent location."

Business Card Purgatory

I present this scenario for people who forget their cards or frequently run out.

> *You are one of five people chosen to explain your business in more detail at a networking event. The rest of the attendees form lines in front of the five of you — each person ready to give business or make a referral to you. All they ask in return is a business card—a nickel or dime memento of your good intentions.*

*The other four people are handing out cards and re-
ceiving leads fast and furiously.*

*You have nothing to share. You had already given out
the five cards you brought. The people in your line are
getting restless. They want to do business with you.
What's the hold up?*

*You are becoming tense. Beads of perspiration are form-
ing on your brow.*

*The troops are getting more and more restless. The other
lines are thinning out. Yours hasn't moved an inch.
Dare they become line-switchers? Do they give their
business to the others?*

*Streams of perspiration are now running down your
face. Your shirt/blouse has few dry spots. Your palms
are wet. Someone must have turned up the heat.*

Your line, too, thins out. Then everyone leaves.

For the lack of a card, the business was lost!

Where Do I Keep Them?

The overall goal, no matter where you choose to keep your
cards at an event, is to look professional and organized. One
option, if you are wearing a jacket or trousers with pockets,
is to keep your business cards in one pocket and the ones you
receive in the other. You may choose to keep your cards in
the same pocket as your hand preference since you usually
reach for your card with that hand.

That option doesn't work for me since as a professional
presenter, I want my suits to fit as nearly perfectly as possible ... which means I don't cut open the pockets. This

necessitates carrying a small purse. Most men I know usually carry their own cards in their inside suit jacket pocket or shirt pocket (when they don't have a jacket on) and put the ones they receive in a trouser pocket.

Another option is put your own cards, at least, behind your nametag if it is one of those plastic holders. This, again, doesn't work for me since my card is a fold-over on a heavy stock, and a supply of them doesn't fit there.

The reason for segregating cards is to make certain you *never* pull out someone else's card to present as yours. This is a major networking sin! Another act you should do penance for is when you give away one of your own cards on which you have written valuable information about someone else.

> *Patricia was in the habit of jotting a personal reminder on business cards. Otis had forgotten his cards, so he wrote his name and phone number on the back of her card. As Otis walked away, Patricia mused to herself that his nose was the reminder she needed to remember him. She quickly jotted "big nose" on his card, put it back in her pocket and went on her way. She was not in the habit of segregating her cards, so, you guessed it; she gave away the card with Otis' information—and her note—on it. She's never done it again!*

Speaking of jotting down reminders, make sure you always have a pen handy. And, women, that means never rooting around in your handbag. Not only is it unprofessional and time-consuming, it could be embarrassing. You never know what you might pull out, or what might fall out!

Replenish your business card supply as soon as you get back to the office. Failing to do so is why so many people have to make up excuses later.

**Replenish your business card supply as soon as
you get back to the office.**

Keep an extra supply of business cards in your glove compartment. It can get you out of jams on Saturday morning grocery trips and Saturday evening "strictly social" events. You never know where your prospects are waiting!

Women, if you will be carrying an evening bag to a formal affair, ask your significant other if it is a man, to carry your business cards in an inside suit jacket pocket.

Read Business Cards When You Get Them

It is proper protocol to pause and read someone's card as soon as you get it. *Never* just glance at the card and then quickly shove it into your pocket. The silence while you are reading each other's cards is an accepted part of the communication process. Use the time to:

- ◆ Review the person's name.
- ◆ Check the person's title.
- ◆ Memorize the name of the business.
- ◆ Check the location of the business.
- ◆ Learn more about nature of the business, if available.

Taking time to read cards and then commenting on any part of them shows other people you are interested and want to learn more about them. It's disappointing—and unforgivable—to put someone's card in your pocket and then ask:

- ◆ "What do you do?"
- ◆ "Where is your business located?"

Practice Good Etiquette

It's proper to exchange cards as soon as you meet. However, if you have not done so and want the other person to have your card, ask for his/her card first.

Asking the other person can also be a graceful way to end a conversation. (More on how to end conversations in Chapter 15.) It's courteous and enables you to combine the process with "I'll call to set up an appointment," or "Thanks, I'll keep your name on file for when I need xxx. "

Err on the side of not giving out your cards if there is even the slightest question about its propriety. The most flagrant abuse I saw was at a networking event in the Southwest Chicago area.

During a speaker's presentation, I noticed one man going from table to table, crouching down and whispering into one person's ear. I was curious, until I received a tap on the back from him. He handed me a stack of his business cards and asked if I would distribute them to each person at my table. After giving him a questioning look, I turned my attention back to the speaker.

Not only was he a distraction, he never even asked for my card or anyone else's in return! I threw the cards in a wastebasket on my way out. If I had kept even one, the temptation would be too great to single him out by name for the reprehensible way he had acted.

Keep Track

At the time of the event, you may think you'll never forget any people you have talked with or where you met them. Yet it's almost impossible not to!

As soon as possible, date your cards in the upper right-hand or left-hand corners. List the function and any other descriptive phrase that will jog your memory. Also jot down if you promised to call or to send something—neglecting to follow up is unforgivable.

File the cards manually, or add the information to your computer before they get lost or buried on your desk. Indefatigables—take note, and do it immediately. You are known for having lost business because you can't find someone's card. One Indefatigable forgot to remove cards from his jeans pocket and couldn't read the blurred ink after he washed the pants!

Go for Quality, Not Quantity

Different people hear this message differently.

Larry, a Careful networker, believes that it is okay to leave an event with only one card so long as it belongs to a potential client.

Corey, an Indefatigable person, likes to leave networking events with his pocket bulging with cards, at least 40 to 50 of them. He believes, to get quality, you must first get quantity.

Do what works for you. Be satisfied if you get one or two good prospects from two hours of networking. The next day, or at least within a few weeks, weed out the ones that are not panning out. A bulging card or address file does not equate with success.

A bulging card or address file does not equate with success.

Follow Up

First of all, do what you promised. Send e-mail, a letter, your promotional materials, or the newspaper / magazine article you promised or make the phone call—within a week. There is no excuse not to do so. Let others know you are sincere and trustworthy.

I highly recommend e-mails for a general "nice to meet you" because of their ease and timeliness. A personal, handwritten note is by far the number one choice for a special "thank you" or an "especially nice to meet you" effect. See Chapter 16 for more hints on staying in touch.

I value sincerity. If I truly enjoyed the person and would like to see them again, even if it does not involve immediate business for either of us, I may call or write for no other reason than to say, "Nice meeting you. Let's stay in touch." If not, I will file the card and wait until I need or can recommend his/her services before I follow up.

chapter 14

The Impact of Endorsements

Now that you know who you are and where you are going and have powerful selling tools in the form of your verbal and printed business cards, you are ready to tackle the actual relationship-building process. One of the things you want to seek and give to others is a personal endorsement of products or services.

Testimonials are one of the strongest selling tools. It is far more impressive for someone else to tell a prospective client that you are an outstanding interior designer than for you to tell them so yourself. Some people have difficulty "bragging" about themselves; others sound too boastful.

It is far more impressive for someone else
to tell a prospective client that you are an
outstanding interior designer than for you to
tell them so yourself.

The reputation and status of the people in your network are key. The more successful, respected and influential your web, the more their endorsements mean to others—and for you.

Do not take the endorsement process lightly. Every time you give one, your reputation ... and your network ... are on the line. It is best to personally experience the product or service you are recommending. In lieu of that, it is suggested that you highly respect the person who gave you the first-hand recommendation.

On a listserve I subscribe to, I saw mention of someone who, with a partner, is coming out with a book in the relationship-building arena. I checked out the website and then sent an e-mail to the woman congratulating her efforts and telling her how I was looking forward to her book.

She replied with a "thank you," and then asked me if I knew groups that were looking for a speaker on the subject. My reply was that I always hear people speak before I recommend them or that I have an endorsement from someone I highly respect. I offered to attend one of her events since she is in the Chicago area. She never replied ... an interesting twist for someone trying to build a reputation in the relationship-building field.

Let's take a closer look at types of endorsements and how you can give and use them most beneficially.

Verbal Endorsements

There are two major types of "spoken" endorsements: in-person and indirect.

In-Person

Someone recommends your product or service to another person(s) during conversation or a speech, workshop or seminar. The impact varies with the reputation of the endorser and how those hearing him/her relate to the person. Another key factor is whether the hearer is in need of what you are selling. The option also always exists for him/her to refer you to someone else. The impact is greater if you are present when the recommendation is given and immediately take charge of further interactions.

Indirect—Permission to Use Name

Another form of verbal endorsement is when satisfied customers or clients give you permission to use their names to contact their networks.

> *"Alice, this is Lillian Bjorseth. John Doe suggested I contact you since you are in charge of this year's programs for the Midwest Society of Professional Consultants."*

This is an excellent way to break the ice. Again, dependent on the referrer's reputation and status, it may be a sure-fire way for you to get an appointment or at least the opportunity to refer people to your website or to send your materials ... where you can again use the referrer's name in a cover letter.

Always state your name before using the name of the referrer. Failure to do so shows disrespect for the person you are calling and a lack of confidence in yourself and what you do.

I give an automatic first strike to people who fail to introduce themselves before beginning to speak. Frequently, these are cold calls, and the callers immediately reduce their chances for a sale to me.

Choose wisely whom you allow to use your name; otherwise, your reputation and influence will dissipate quickly.

Another form of an indirect referral is when you know other people well enough that you are sure they will be willing to talk with someone else, even without your first checking with them.

> When I owned my business leads organization, Phyllis, a psychotherapist, called for membership information and also asked if she could speak with another psychotherapist who was a member. I referred her to Lynn, whom I was confident would be candid and praiseworthy of BBC. Phyllis chose to join and to help start a new chapter. Because I had spent time building a relationship with Lynn, I was confident I could use her as a reference without first consulting her. Of course, I thanked her later and made sure it would be okay to use her name again.

People like Lynn are what I refer to as oak trees in your network. You have such a solid relationship with them, i.e., the roots are so deep and strong, that you inherently know they will respond positively. You undoubtedly have a few people like that in your network, people whom you don't have to call before you use their name. As a courtesy, let them know as soon as possible that someone may be calling them (has called them) and thank them for the endorsement.

Remember that oak trees started out as acorns (seeds). To develop these kind of relationships takes lots of TCC—time, care and commitment. Choose your oak tree relationships wisely so that your efforts will not go for naught. It can be disappointing to build this kind of bond, only to find the person is not necessarily worth all that effort.

Written Endorsements

This category includes three formats: letters of recommendation, client list and quotes. You may have to exert more energy because it takes more effort to get someone to "put it in writing."

Letters of Recommendation

Complimentary letters are a mainstay of my promotional package and carry a lot of weight with potential clients. No one likes to hire a trainer or speaker "cold." It could be disastrous. While my videotape is a good introduction, I have found that many "potentials" have turned into "actuals" (with more conviction) by reading my letters of recommendation.

The ideal recommendation is an unsolicited thank-you letter. However, it is okay to ask a satisfied client to "put it in writing." Some people may not be accustomed to doing so, and without your urging, would not even think of it. The following letter (it was the client's suggestion to write it) is included with permission from Lance Vandenbroek, who at the time was training manager, United Airlines Employees Credit Union.

Dear Lillian:

I just wanted to drop you a line to let you know how much we enjoyed your recent presentation of the workshop Improve Your PeopleSmarts. *I have had a number of conversations with those who attended, and to a person they felt that the program gave them a much better understanding of what makes them and their co-workers "tick." Each person I spoke with agreed that the knowledge they gained from the workshop would improve their interpersonal skills and make them more effective team members both interdepartmentally and intradepartmentally.*

> *At United Airlines Employees' Credit Union, we are very careful about the way we use our training budget and expect a sizeable return on investment for every program we offer. I can without hesitation affirm that the cost of bringing this program to our employees was money very well spent.*
>
> *Should you wish to use me as a reference for other organizations that are contemplating hiring you to present this workshop, please do so with confidence that I will repeat this well-deserved praise.*

I have also included a variety of endorsements on my website, featuring specific ones for coaching, training, speaking and my products on the corresponding pages.

Client List

Another good endorsement is to include a list of clients in your promotional package. Go a step further—include a contact name, address, and phone or fax number and e-mail address so the potential client can reach them easily. In advance, get permission from each client to make sure that he / she is willing to spend time promoting you.

This can be a good alternative if you have successfully worked for a company that has a policy against written letters of recommendation but will allow verbal endorsements.

Quotes

Using quotes from satisfied customers can be an expeditious way to show the variety of companies / individuals with which you have worked. You can include them in a company brochure or your website.

In any case, play it safe and get permission to use a quote. A verbal okay may be fine. The safest bet is to get it in writing ... e-mail works well for that.

Depending on your audiences, you may wish to collect a variety of endorsements so you can use specific ones to reach certain audiences, i.e., letters from associations where you keynoted or presented a workshop to use when you are marketing to other associations.

It's my experience that executives I coach are not comfortable with giving me a written testimonial; however, to a person they always offer to speak with anyone I refer to them for a verbal endorsement.

Use the suggestions given here to implement a verbal and written endorsement program for yourself and for people in your network. Offer to do the latter before they ask! This "added service" will go a long way toward building oak-tree relationships.

chapter 15

How to Really Work a Room

People tell me they understand the value of networking. Yet, they have trouble getting over the first hurdle: walking into a roomful of strangers and feeling as if they fit, as if they were meant to be there. People complain of feeling overwhelmed, rejected, left out, like a fifth wheel—at least for the first 10 to 15 minutes. Some people feel this way every time a conversation ends, and they need to start the process anew.

Compare it to jumping into a swimming pool of cold water: Just do it! You know it will warm up once you are in. This chapter is loaded with tips to take away the coldness, fear and rejection, and replace them with confidence, warmth and enthusiasm.

One of the major reasons I created my newest product, *52 Ways To Break The Ice & Target Your Market,* is to help people alleviate that fear and pain that is so real for the more than half of the world who is introverted. It's not enough just to meet people either; you need to make the interaction meaningful and yourself memorable to make the connection worthwhile.

It's up to you! If, and when, you choose to take the initiative to "work a room" … my suggestions will make it easier for you.

Pretend that roomfuls of strangers are guests in your home. What would you do? Welcome them, of course. Do the same thing in your business life. I learned this principle from my long-time friend, Janet Asbury, when we spent time on the singles scene. When we went to a lounge, she would say:

> *"Pretend we have been invited to a party in someone's home. When we arrive, many of the guests will be strangers. Our goal will be to meet them, so we'll feel comfortable. When we leave, we'll have made new friends."*

We had fun making new friends! I never felt isolated or alone even if I arrived at our destination ahead of her or other friends. Later, when I started a singles organization, I slid easily into the role of envisioning each of the attendees as my special guest. I welcomed them, and then introduced each to other attendees. I made sure no one was ever alone.

This same methodology works in the business world. Let's walk through it step by step.

Arrive Early

This is a major point many people overlook. The key people (except maybe the very top honchos) are there early. Many build in time to welcome guests who come early—be one of those who takes advantage of this pre-time. This is an opportunity to shake hands, make a good impression and set the stage for you to introduce the organizers to guests later. Others may be impressed because *you* know the movers and shakers of the event. (Remember, what we said earlier about meeting the *right* people.)

One caveat, though, don't launch into a long conversation as the sponsors may have last-minute details to handle.

> *Frequently, when I speak at a luncheon or dinner or keynote a conference, I arrive early to check out the facilities, set up my display and "get into the moment." While I enjoy people coming by to say "Hello and welcome," I can't concentrate on full-blown interactions at this point.*

Arriving early also gives you the chance to scope the room and strategically position yourself or your materials. Here are some things to check out:

♦ Where to sit for a good, open view of the podium

♦ Where to stand to see guests arriving or departing

♦ How to get the best exposure for your materials on the networking table

♦ Whether the food's out early

If the food is ready, eat as soon as you arrive, or wait until the end. Sitting down to eat limits the number of people you will meet. Carrying a plate with you is preferable to sitting but can be an impediment to shaking hands and can get downright messy, depending on the food. (Chicken wings are particularly bad!) Any spots on ties, blouses or shirts must be removed immediately. Indefatigables, you are particularly vulnerable to spilling on yourself and others since you are so animated ... even when you are listening! Of course, it is impolite to speak with your mouth full. Circulating with your hands (and mouth) empty is preferable. Women, a shoulder bag is far more practical than carrying a clutch purse.

Imbibe in alcoholic drinks only if you are sure it will not impede your purpose for being there. Know your limit.

Overindulging is unfathomable at a business networking event. You may not remember what you did; however, others will!

Greet Other People

As people begin arriving, approach them. Help them feel welcome just as you were made to feel earlier. You already have some of the inside information since you were among the first to be there. Throughout the evening, keep your eyes peeled for people who are alone. Make them your special concern. It will give you a reason to continually meet new people.

John, an Indefatigable type, is a sales trainer who always made it a point at business receptions to keep an eye out for anyone who was standing alone. He hit pay dirt for his own business when one of the people he greeted happened to be regional sales manager for a Fortune 500 company.

He told this story over and over to other trainers at one of his industry's professional organizations. He caught the ear of a staff member who gave him a slot at the next national conference to talk about the benefits of networking. That meeting, in turn, was covered by a national business magazine, which interviewed him for an article on effective marketing techniques.

And, as John likes to say, "It all started with an alert eye and a handshake."

Introduce Contacts to One Another

Again, just as you would in your home, introduce the people you know to one another. You become a catalyst for helping others meet new prospects and friends. Along with the introduction, give a sentence or two of information about the person so that the two (or more) people who have just met have a jumping-off point.

Weave Newcomers Into the Conversation

As soon as possible, weave a new person into the conversation. An easy way to do this is to quickly review what you were talking about and ask his/her opinion.

Devote your time to pulling people into conversations rather than expecting them to listen to you. Others will be grateful that you helped them feel more comfortable. The rewards for you will come—maybe a little later or in ways you never dreamed of—but they will come.

**Devote your time to pulling people
into conversations rather than
expecting them to listen to you.**

"You can have everything you want in life if you will just help enough people get what they want."
—Zig Ziglar

My 10-Minute Rule

While quantity does not necessarily equal quality, networking is a numbers game, particularly at an event where you do not know many of the people. Meeting ten people versus five assures you more chances of "connecting" with the right one. A good rule is to meet at least ten people during a two-hour event. That equates to about ten minutes each, given registration time, organizers' remarks and other activities.

Hence, I have developed the 10-Minute Rule for Working a Room. I've divided the time slot into three parts: the introduction, the body and the conclusion. This gives you time for small talk, at least five minutes for a solid business exchange and another couple of minutes to lay the groundwork for saying good-bye. If you spent 20 minutes with someone, try to shorten the next couple of encounters to make up the time. Ten minutes is good for planting seeds—not harvesting the crop—and that's what networking is all about. (Harvesting is sales and, of course, can take months, even years.)

**Ten minutes is good for planting seeds—
not harvesting the crop—and that's what
networking is all about.**

The Introduction

This segment typically begins with small talk, which may be a misnomer since it plays such an important part in the relationship-building process. Small talk is the necessary prelude to future meaningful conversations ... and business opportunities. It's what we use to break the ice when we meet someone new or someone we know casually.

Ironically, this is the most fearful part of the conversation for most people, and we immediately have a major challenge to overcome. Men have a few preferred topics in their small talk repertoire:

- ◆ Sports
- ◆ Current events
- ◆ Politics
- ◆ Business/jobs

Women, on the other hand, have an endless array of top-ics—hundreds, it seems—they are comfortable with, and many of them involve family and home.

Men need to be more accepting of women's desires to re-late through communication and of their desires to talk about family. Women need to respect men's desires not to discuss personal issues at length and bone up on sports and current events so comments from both will mesh and turn into help-ful conversations for both. (See Chapter 18 for more helpful hints on understanding and overcoming gender differences in communication.)

> *Years ago, at a male-dominated executive breakfast club meeting (about 375 men and 25 women), I joined two men at a table. Their conversation was impersonal, and they showed no interest in me or what I did. I played their game.*

> *Another woman joined us, sitting down across the table from one of the men. I smiled and said, "Hi." The men ignored her. She said nothing until one of the men re-marked it was a shame that the scheduled speaker, Winston Churchill III, had to cancel because of a late vote in Parliament. The woman then said, "Yeah, he could have given us the real story about Charles and Di."*

> *Silence. Then one of the men said, "Who cares about Charles and Di?" The woman lowered her head and never spoke again.*

Even today, men's preferences still set the stage at events that involve both genders. Ideally, the future will see give-and-take on both sides.

The introductory period can also be a good time to ex-change business cards; however, it is not necessary to do so immediately. Remember, if you want someone to have your card, it is protocol for you to ask them for their card first.

Here are some techniques to help you make the introductory period even more successful.

Remember People's Names—One of the keys to any relationship-building situation is to remember other people's names. Although nametags help, you cannot always rely on them. Some people wear them on the "other" side (the right side is the correct place), or the tags might be obstructed by clothing or partially hidden as people move their hands and bodies during conversations. People who are farsighted and don't wear their corrective lenses can't even read nametags.

To help you remember names:

◆ Take a good look at a nametag (when one is worn and you can read it!) immediately upon meeting the person.

◆ Choose a prominent feature about the person—hair color, earrings, mustache, eyes—and associate it with the person's name: Linda, platinum hair; Lois, large gold hoop earrings; Phil, handlebar mustache; Wayne, piercing blue eyes.

◆ Repeat the person's first name several times during the first few minutes of the conversation. Use it occasionally throughout.

◆ *Study* the person's business card. Inscribe the name to memory.

◆ Repeat the name when ending the conversation.

In Case You Forget—And you will forget if you have any of these common listening blocks:

◆ Judging

◆ Preoccupation

◆ Daydreaming

◆ Lack of interest

Whatever the reason, you need to do something right away to lessen and erase the tension. (If you are talking one-on-one, you might slip by until a third person joins the conversation and the introduction process is repeated.) Adapt these hints to your situation:

◆ Dart a quick glance at the person's nametag, when available.

◆ Be honest and say you forgot.

◆ Make an opening remark like: "Joe, glad you joined us. We are discussing health care reform. Do the two of you know each other?" Then pause. It is likely the two will introduce each other—and save you from embarrassment.

◆ Make a joke. "They say memory is the first thing to go, and mine seems to be heading south! What is your name again?" or "I'm sorry. I've misfiled your name is my memory bank."

◆ Help others. When you notice someone pausing when introducing you, extend your hand and say your name. They will appreciate it, too!

Introduction Mechanics—Even though we learned introduction etiquette in elementary and high school English classes, we may not remember who is introduced to whom. Here's a refresher:

◆ A younger person is introduced to an older person

◆ A man is introduced to a woman

◆ A less important person is introduced to a VIP

An easy way to recall the procedure is this: You say the name of the person who is older, the woman, and the more important person first:

"Dad, I would like you to meet Joe Somebody, an associate of mine. Joe, this is my dad, Charlie Bingenheimer."

"This is Mary Someone, president of the auxiliary. I'd like you to meet Jill Everyone, who is visiting our meeting tonight."

Include a person's full name and the person's affiliation, if you can fit it in.

When introducing yourself, *always* say your first and last name, even if you are wearing a nametag. People may not be able to see the tag, or even if they can, they may not know how to pronounce it. With a name like Bjorseth (B-or-seth), I know all about that!

Don't Assume Nicknames—Just because someone's name is Robert doesn't mean he wants to be called Bob. All Michaels don't like the shortened version, "Mike."

Your name is the most personal thing you own. You deserve to be addressed as you want to be; however, you must let people know your preference.

Let people's nametags and business cards be your first guide. If someone's card has "Robert" on it and his nametag says "Bob," you are safe going with "Bob." If he uses "Robert" on both, let that be your guide. If your preprinted name badge differs from your choice, lightly cross out "Robert" and write "Bob" on it. Use a felt tip pen so people can read it.

Some names may not be as obvious. I always use Lillian. Periodically, someone asks, "I assume it's okay to call you Lil?" or "Do you go by Lilly?" In both cases, I reply, "No." My lack of infatuation with those nicknames goes back to childhood when as the youngest of four sisters, I was called Baby Lil or Baby Lilly. Let people know through your personal use and your nametag how you want to be addressed.

It's okay for you to be persistent. It's your name!

The Body

The goal here is to find a commonality. Once that is attained, the rest of the conversation flows easily because people relax more quickly with people with whom they have something in common. It also feels as if you have overcome a major hurdle and everything is downhill from here.

So how do you make that magical commonality appear? The answer is through probing, a listening technique that encourages you to ask questions and then remain quiet and pay attention.

In this me-centered society, most of us want to know what the person we have just met can do for us. Bury that urge or at least hide it under a basket for awhile. Instead, follow Dale Carnegie's sage advice:

> *"You can close more business in two months by becoming interested in other people than you can in two years by trying to get people interested in you."*

Another golden rule is to ask open-ended questions. Do everything you can to avoid the following kind of conversation:

> *"Is this your first time here?" "Yes."*

> *"Did you have trouble finding it?" "No."*

> *"Was the traffic bad?" "Yes."*

Soon that awful, painful Silence reigns again.

Consider using our **ICE BREAKERS** (described in Chapter 22). These pre-set questions help start conversations and are useful, interesting and entertaining to newcomers and veterans at any kind of event.

The next step is to ask questions especially tailored to the other person's responses to previous ones. An astute communicator and networker will note you are asking a lot of questions and return the favor. It's easy to get most people to open up (you have to work hardest on Careful styles). Encourage people to voice their opinions or elaborate. Ask questions like:

◆ "What do you do?"

◆ "Who's a good prospect for you?"

◆ "How can I help you with . . . ?"

◆ "What do you enjoy most about being a member of …?"

◆ "Are you a member of this organization?" If yes, then:
  • "What is the best feature of this group?"
  • "Why did you join?"
  • "What could I gain by joining?"

Even though these questions are listed in rapid-fire order, don't feel as if you need to ask them like this. Be thoughtful and considerate and don't make people feel as it they are being bombarded. No one reacts well to that. Allow time for reflection, pauses and analysis in the conversation. Sometimes, just one good question can spark a conversation that will go on and on.

(For individuals … during receptions preceding conferences, meetings and meals, refer to our pre-printed **ICE BREAKERS,** described in Chapter 22. For a meeting or workshop setting … check out our "Find Common Ground" ice breaker exercise in Chapter 23.)

Non-threatening subjects include:

◆ Favorite sport, movie, television show, book

◆ Birthplace

◆ High school / college attended

◆ Vacation spot

◆ Non-religious holiday traditions

When You Do Speak About Yourself—Choose topics relevant or interesting to the person(s) you are with. Listen carefully and base your topics on what has been or is being said. Also consider other people's occupations. Be flexible, and adapt to the moment.

> **What to Do:** *John met Marie at an industry dinner. During the networking hour, he heard her say that she was trying to close a sale with a potential client in England. When he found himself seated next to her at dinner, he took the opportunity to tell her about his business trips to England for a former employer. He shared insights into how the British do business. She listened intently, and asked a lot of questions. John also asked questions so he could gear his remarks even more closely to her work.*

> **What not to Do:** *Vickie smiled to herself as she excused herself from her conversation with Joe and Harvey. "If you could call it a conversation," she thought to herself. She had never witnessed such disjointed remarks and one-upmanship. Both men had separate agendas. Joe kept talking about his sales promotion business, and Harvey replied with comments about his insurance practice. Their responses were self-serving and neither was benefiting from their time together. Vickie doubted she would be missed! No one had even asked what her business was even though she had inquired about theirs.*

Watch the "I" overkill. "I" is the 24th most frequently used word in the English language. Arthur Pleninger, author of *How To Survive and Market Yourself in Management,* calls it

> *"... the most reprehensible word in the English language . . . heavily overused, and worse yet, it conveys a self-centered, self-concerned attitude."*

Entrepreneurs and small business owners can say "we, us, our" to eliminate overuse of "I" when talking about their companies. In fact, the more "you's" you can incorporate into your conversations and correspondence, the more empathetic it will be—and the more relevant and interesting it will be to others.

The Conclusion

Many people are so concerned with attending events alone, entering a roomful of strangers and breaking the ice that they give no thought to extricating themselves from a conversation. "Getting stuck" with one or two people can greatly diminish the benefits of your two hours of attempted seed planting. And it can be boring and irritating ... for all involved.

End It Upbeat—Plan and rehearse (if necessary) your exit statements. They can be as important as your introductory remarks. Knowing when and how to use them also is vital. Make the tone upbeat to leave a lasting good impression. Stay a few minutes longer rather than cut someone off and leave a sour taste.

Indefatigables, help others by observing the ten-minute rule yourself and by curtailing your tales. If you are dealing with an Indefatigable—you may have to be more obvious in your endings. Sometimes, they just don't get it, especially if you are being subtle!

When to do it:

◆ After about 10 minutes

◆ When the other person's eyes noticeably begin wandering around the room

◆ When others shift their stance toward other people or the door

◆ When the conversation lags

◆ When the other person repeatedly says "interesting," "hmmm," "really," (nothing words), especially in a monotone response

How to do it:

◆ Ask for the other person's card, if you do not yet have it.

◆ Set up a time to call or meet with the other person.

◆ Excuse yourself shortly after another person has joined you and others.

◆ Be up front.

  • "It's been nice talking with you and . . ."

  • "I see the client I invited has just arrived."

  • "I will keep your card on file when I need . . ."

  • "I want to meet some of the other people; it's my first time here."

  • "I haven't been here for six months, and I want to rekindle other acquaintances."

  • "I can only stay for an hour, and I have several other people to talk with."

  • "I'd like to continue this conversation. May I call you?"

  • "Would you like to have lunch next week?"

And, when all else fails:

  • "I want to get something else to eat or drink."

Keep in mind what we discussed in Chapter 7 that 93 percent of the message is communicated through "how" we say it, not "what" we say. Therefore, your body language and vocal tone play a far more important part in your closing than do the words themselves.

Adapt these suggestions to your style, and you are bound to make a favorable impression.

Say Good-Bye to Everyone You Met

Plan time in your schedule to spend a minute or two saying good-bye to everyone you met. First and last impressions have the most impact. Keep the last words short, upbeat and positive and always use the person's first name (which you will have remembered!):

◆ "Kelly, it was nice meeting you. I'll call you Thursday."

◆ "Bob, thanks again for the tip on the stock market."

◆ "Mary, I'll call tomorrow to set up a lunch meeting."

◆ "Ken, I'll call my associate tomorrow to tell him how you can help him with his current challenge."

chapter **16**

How to Stay in Touch

Y ou've met new contacts, you have a file full of new business cards. Now, what do you do? You stay in touch, of
course. Myriad ways exist ... what is important is that you
do it and that you choose the most effective method for the
situation. As we examine the various ways, we'll put special
emphasis again on understanding the other person's behavioral style, this time as to how you can recognize and best
respond to them in Cyberspace and on the telephone. While
it may require some behavioral modification on your part, it
may also more quickly lead to win-win solutions that help
you get the job or the business.

Tools for staying in touch include one-on-one and mass
communication devices. Except for newsletters and e-zines,
none of them requires a lot of time, and they are well worth

every minute you spent. Newsletters and e-zines, too, can be worth their time in gold because of the number of people you can reach with a relatively personal message and because of their built-in longevity.

Handwritten Notes

Whether it's business or social communications, the personal touch is the most heartfelt and sincere on your part and the most warmly and sincerely received. Taking the time to jot a personal note means you care enough to compose a message just for the person who is receiving it. Because hand writing usually takes more effort than typing, it also shows you are willing to go an extra mile to send a message.

> *When I helped Sue get a job at a large bank by referring her to an executive recruiter, I received two handwritten notes from her: one telling me how the process was going and another when she was chosen from among 12 candidates. The notes were an extra, personal touch in addition to a phone call. They showed me her appreciation.*

Is your handwriting hard to read? You're not alone! People will spend extra time deciphering it when they know you have said something nice. On your part, slow down and do your best. Take a few extra minutes to make it intelligible. You can do it. Think of the appreciation on the other end and the good that will come of it. Hand address the envelope, too. Both need to be done in the same manner to be effective. Don't use pre-printed return labels!

You can have note cards custom-designed to coordinate with your company's printed image or you can use preprinted ones with messages, such as "Thank you for your extra effort," "Thanks for your business," "Thanks for the referrals" or just "Thank you." All of them have blank space for you to write your personalized message.

E-mail

Staying in touch via e-mail is unequivocally the easiest and fastest method. Even the telephone pales in comparison since, typically, you have to limit your calls to 9-5 pm.

The ease of sending your messages via e-mail also has inherent challenges. Failure to proofread, disregard for grammar and spelling and a response while you are upset are among the most common pitfalls.

I contend another major challenge is lack of human sensitivity. Because people are writing on an inanimate screen they forget that there is a living human being on the receiving end ... someone with needs, desires, wants and experiences that will impact how each message is read. It's much easier to interpret and react when you can read people's body language and hear their tone of voice face-to-face. Building and maintaining relationships in Cyberspace puts an extra onus on the sender and receiver to ensure messages are sent and gotten as they are intended to be received. In other words, the sender often has to work harder on how the message is stated than when saying it over the phone or in person.

The following will help you more easily recognize the sender's natural communication style and help you more clearly understand where he/she is coming from so you can respond more effectively.

How to Recognize Dauntless People Online

Keep in mind their desire for quick, brief, concise, yet purposeful, communication, and that they:

◆ Can be direct (blunt!) with requests (demands!).

◆ Ignore spelling, grammatical errors.

◆ Like short, to-the-point messages.

◆ Seldom use salutations/closings.

◆ Use powerful pre-set signature.

How to Respond to "Ds" Online

♦ Be succinct; get to the point.

♦ Give just the facts, ma'am.

♦ Insure contents are important/relevant to the receiver.

♦ Pose challenges to get quick answers.

♦ Use logic; forget "touchy-feely" words.

How to Recognize Indefatigables Online

Remember their optimistic, enthusiastic, emotional outlook on life, and that they:

♦ Convey emotion and energy, even in Cyberspace.

♦ Create their own meaning for e-mail punctuation.

♦ Generate enthusiasm through words, tone and punctuation.

♦ Get to the point ... eventually.

♦ Rebel against learning how to use computer technology.

How to Respond to "Is" Online

♦ Allow more days than usual for responses below they tend to read and move on, rather than respond in the moment.

♦ Balance e-mail with telephone and face-to-face meetings; they thrive on actually hearing you and seeing the whites of your eyes.

♦ Be friendly, upbeat.

♦ Spell out your message clearly.

How to Recognize Supportive People Online

They appreciate sincerity, warmth and a calm, easy approach, and they:

- ◆ Always use a salutation and closing.
- ◆ Convey sincerity and warmth.
- ◆ Find e-mail a comfortable, safe way to communicate.
- ◆ Involve others through group lists, like sending "copy to."
- ◆ May ask about family and "how things are."

How to Respond to "Ss" Online

- ◆ Give them time to sort out information/respond.
- ◆ "Listen" carefully to what they have to say.
- ◆ Make e-mail resemble business correspondence format.
- ◆ Return sincerity and warmth.
- ◆ Show your appreciation through your words.

How to Recognize Careful People Online

Careful styles are formal, patient and logical, and they:

- ◆ Are accurate in content, grammar, spelling.
- ◆ Know and follow e-mail etiquette.
- ◆ Send long, d e t a i l e d messages, often with attachments, too.
- ◆ Use given name/unpretentious pre-set signature.

How to Respond to "Cs" Online

- ◆ Be as formal as you can.
- ◆ Give details; avoid one-line responses at all costs.
- ◆ Pay attention to grammar/spelling.

- Start with a salutation or at least use their name.

- Use logic; avoid emotional words/tone.

Phone Calls

Personal interaction is powerful and good! Pick up the phone occasionally and talk directly with the people in your network. I'm beginning to see a trend of too-little phone usage ... with the message being that it takes too much time. Sure, you may have to play some "phone tag;" however, it can be well worth the little extra effort.

If you are the initiator, take the clue from the other person, especially if they are your customers. If you leave a voice mail message, and the other person returns it via e-mail, follow suit.

Voice mail continues to be a major communication and relationship- building aid since you can leave your message with your inflection, rate, tone and pitch—delivering it exactly as you want it to be received. Remember, too, that not everyone has a laptop, and when you need to reach somebody who is traveling, the telephone is still your best bet.

When you are on the receiving end of phone calls, return them! I have yet to hear a good, logical reason why a call was not returned, short of a personal or business emergency— and we are talking real emergencies. Failure to return a call immediately makes me suspect of including that person in my network. What happens if they were to do that to someone in my network to whom I referred them?

The following will help you more easily recognize and respond to different communication styles on the telephone.

How to Recognize a Dauntless Person on the Telephone

- Chooses time/date/place to meet

- Dislikes interruptions, yet interrupts

◆ Gets right to the point, may bypass "hello"

◆ Has clear purpose in mind ahead of time; speaks in bullet style

◆ Prefers informal style

◆ Speaks and thinks quickly

◆ Speaks authoritatively, powerfully

◆ Uses logic; avoids emotion

◆ Wants to get own message across, may not listen to other person

How to Respond to Dauntless People on the Telephone

◆ Be clear and succinct.

◆ Be immune to their brusqueness.

◆ Don't give details, unless asked.

◆ End the conversation when they quit responding; undoubtedly, they have moved on to other activities.

◆ Plug your remarks into their goals.

◆ Summarize, summarize, summarize.

How to Recognize an Indefatigable Person on the Telephone

◆ Begins with an upbeat "hello"

◆ Holds side conversations with another person in office / at home while talking on phone, has radio and / or TV on, too

◆ Likes informal style

◆ Shows wide range of emotions through rate, pitch, tone, rhythm, inflection

- Speaks faster and faster as excitement mounts
- Talks about weather, the weekend, vacations, whatever—before getting down to business
- Uses touchy-feely words
- Uses words others can picture

How to Respond to Indefatigable People on the Telephone

- Ask them to repeat if they speak too quickly during an outburst.
- End the conversation—even if they called you.
- Respond quickly when given a chance to speak.
- Set a timer beforehand.
- Signal for time out if they have worn you out.
- Try to get in more than "hello."

How to Recognize a Supportive Person on the Telephone

- Begins with a warm "hello"
- Conveys calm, friendly environment
- Listens well
- Personifies good customer service
- Speaks slowly and carefully
- Thinks before speaking; comfortable with long pauses
- Uses informal style

How to Respond to Supportive People on the Telephone

- Ask about their family.
- Be amicable and sincere.

- Don't demand or push.
- End the conversation if you are the caller.
- Provide information slowly, methodically.
- Refrain from unloading on them; they will listen politely until you're done.

How to Recognize a Careful Person on the Telephone

- Begins formally: "Good morning, Ms. Bjorseth. This is Jean Doe. I am returning your call from Friday."
- Critiques and analyzes what you have said before responding; comfortable with long, silent periods
- Gives you facts rather than opinions
- Keeps it brief
- "Observes" your tone and words to get the message meaning
- Keeps self and personal information out of conversation

How to Respond to Careful People on the Telephone

- Allow them time to analyze.
- Avoid small talk.
- Condense it, yet give pertinent details.
- Don't ask personal questions.
- Don't repeat yourself.
- Have facts in order before you call.
- Keep your personal affairs to yourself.
- Use titles—Dr., Mr., Ms.—unless well acquainted.

Business Meals

Frequently, your e-mail and telephone contact will lead to face-to-face meetings. Whether you choose to have them with breakfast, lunch or dinner, there is etiquette you should follow. Knowing this ahead of time often prevents embarrassing moments during the interchange.

Host's Responsibilities

The host is the person who extends the invitation, even if both of you were discussing the options. It is, therefore, the responsibility of the host to pay the bill, including the tip. Additional duties include:

- Suggest the time/date/place.

- Make the reservation.

- Reconfirm with your guest, preferably a day or two before.

- Pre-arrange a meeting location, either a specific spot inside the restaurant or nearby.

- Offer to pick up your guest if it is convenient for both of you, i.e., you either live or work in the same vicinity.

- Arrive early and make arrangements to pay the check.

- Follow the maitre d' to be seated. Offer your guest the best seat.

- Be familiar with the menu and offer suggestions.

- Don't discuss business until after the meal has been ordered. It helps if you have done your homework and know topics with which he/she is comfortable.

- Ask if your guest has time for dessert.

- Politely take the bill when it is offered and pay with as little attention as possible.

The Role of Guest

As the guest, you also have responsibilities that are just as important. You want to make the host glad he/she invited you. The first thing you need to do is acknowledge the invitation promptly, either confirming or expressing regrets. If the latter, it is proper to provide optional dates to the host. Additional duties include:

♦ Arrive on time. You need to call if you'll be even slightly late—either the restaurant or the host (make arrangements ahead of time to have your host's cell phone number and for him/her to have yours).

♦ Follow your host to be seated and take the chair that is offered.

♦ Listen to the host's suggestion and then make your choice. It is not essential that you take one of the offered selections; however, it is vital that you do not choose one of the most expensive items on the menu. This ends up making you look cheap.

♦ Do not offer to pay or leave a tip.

♦ Thank your host; send a formal note or a small gift, as is fitting.

♦ Return the favor, depending on the nature of your relationship.

Letters and Memos

Even in this fast-paced audio and visual world, we still need to "put it in writing" occasionally for effectiveness, expediency or for the record.

There's no magic to business writing; it's simply good writing. Brevity, clarity and good grammar are important. Written communication, as we discussed in Chapter 10, is often the first impression you make on others. You want it to be believable, meaningful and persuasive. You want your personality to show through so the reader can "hear" you and understand your message.

Some people fear putting it on paper—to the point they break out in a sweat as they look at the blank computer screen or piece of paper. Consequently, they put off memos and letters—sometimes, so long the written documents no longer are effective.

Proposals are often requested and must be submitted in writing. Personal cover letters must accompany any promotional materials or resumés you sent. Communicating with many people simultaneously is safest and most effective when done in writing. Everyone gets the same message.

Our audiotape and workbook, *Write Right*, will help you free up your creative process and get your ideas flowing.

Articles and Clippings

Sending a client, customer or employer (or a prospective one) a relevant, useful article, photo, cartoon or anecdote from a magazine, newspaper or newsletter is one of the easiest ways to show others you care. First of all, you listened carefully enough to know what their business, personal or social interests are. Second, you took the time to clip it and/or send it via mail, fax or e-mail. All that is needed is a short, handwritten note such as:

> *"Bill, FYI. Lillian."*

> *"Bill, I thought you might find this information helpful. Lillian."*

My associates and friends frequently send me cartoons since they know I like to use them in my presentations. I reciprocate by watching for articles that are relevant to their business. It's like having extra sets of eyes and subscribing to more publications without the effort or cost.

Sending clips via e-mail, fax or the mail is also a great way to keep your name in front of clients or prospects—who will file the information if it is relevant. The day they use it—or just happen to pull it out of the file—is the day your name reappears with no extra effort on your part.

Newsletters/E-Zines

A newsletter, whether in print, or an e-zine sent via e-mail, is an excellent vehicle to assist you in your relationship-building activities. You can publish one if you are a soloist or if you are part of a multibillion-dollar corporation—whether you work out of your home or in a 100-story office complex.

Before you begin writing, consider what you want to accomplish, who your audience is, how the costs compare to your budget and what the content will be.

Define the Purpose

- ◆ Educate/inform
- ◆ Interest prospects
- ◆ Replace other collateral materials
- ◆ Retain current clients
- ◆ Use as handout or giveaway to find a job

Target the Market

- ◆ Current clients
- ◆ Future clients
  - • Number of employees
  - • Revenues
- ◆ Professional associates
- ◆ Prospective employers

Determine the Budget (Many of these apply only to the printed version.)

- Design

- Writing

- Mailing list

- Preparation of mailing

- Bulk mail permit

- Postage

- Press run

- Frequency

Decide on Content

- News

  - Awards / recognition

  - Columns / internal, guest

  - Current search areas

  - New address / location / hours

  - New products / seminars

  - Policy changes

  - Previous job experience

  - Seminars / presentations / classes

  - Staff promotions

- Industry information

  - History

  - Issues / regulations

  - Market trends

  - New technology

- ◆ Testimonials
  - Case histories
  - Efficiency
  - Money saved
  - Problems solved
  - Quotes
- ◆ Miscellaneous
  - Artwork
  - Cartoons
  - Coupons, questionnaires
  - Incentives
  - Potpourri
  - Trivia quizzes

A newsletter can add a professional touch to your networking. It can:

- ◆ add prestige to your business.
- ◆ boost employee morale.
- ◆ build credibility for your company.
- ◆ enhance *your* sense of pride.
- ◆ give a sense of accomplishment.
- ◆ highlight market goals.
- ◆ let you share / renew passion for your business.
- ◆ provide a forum to update customers.
- ◆ provide an editorial platform.

chapter 17

Why Media Attention Helps

A local library hired me to do a two-part Saturday morning program on "Breakthrough Networking." The library arranged for two local newspapers to interview me ahead of time.

B ecause of a newspaper article . . .

The president of the advisory committee of a well-known high-technology forum who lives in the same town read about the program. He asked me to speak at the forum's semi-annual networking event six weeks later, also offering me the opportunity to exhibit my materials and products. A speech was born.

Because of the speech and exhibit . . .

> *Attendees at the networking event stopped by my exhibit, requesting more information about my business leads organization (I owned at the time), my products and programs.*

. . . several people joined my networking organization and referred me as a speaker.

Media publicity was one of the major ingredients in my initial marketing plan for Duoforce Enterprises and unequivocally remains one of the reasons for its success and growth.

Having your name in the news is a way to gain recognition before people have met you. In fact, it also builds trust for you as a person and your business. General public opinion is that you must be considered an expert in your field for the media to choose to interview and feature you.

> *When I received a call from the human resources department (HR) of a local company to facilitate a discussion on the importance of good communication at a strategic planning session, I found out later that the president years earlier had cut out a notice in the newspaper about me. My name was familiar to him when HR suggested the company hire me.*

How Do You Get Publicity?

First and foremost, publicity is *free*. You don't pay a penny to have a media release appear in a newspaper; and, therefore, the media has the final say as to whether to edit your material, and if, when and where to run it. Likewise, it doesn't cost you anything to be interviewed in the electronic media. That makes it imperative that you know how to deal with the media effectively.

First and foremost, publicity is *free.*

The primary way to let print and electronic media know what you have to offer is through a media release. The release must be built around a news peg —an award, an event, a product announcement, a relocation—to make it newsworthy. Editors and producers decide whether the materials are timely and of interest to their listeners, readers or viewers.

Editors, like all of us, are busy and appreciate those who help fill their pages and the airwaves more easily. Just as quickly, though, they tend to shun those who just "take up their time."

> *A former newspaper business editor shared with me that he would get hundreds of releases a day via mail, the fax and e-mail. Some of them he routinely discarded by looking at the return address on the envelope or the fax or e-mail address. From experience, he had learned that while these people routinely sent releases, they just as routinely failed to build them around a news peg.*

Saying that you own a jewelry store is not newsworthy if you have been in business at the same location for years and are not offering anything new. What can make it newsworthy is

◆ moving to a new location.

◆ having a famous jewelry collection on display for several weeks.

◆ donating 10 percent of sales during the Christmas holidays to your favorite charity.

Sending a press release stating that you are a financial services adviser is not newsworthy. What is news is that you

- have earned membership in your agency's million dollar club.

- were the top producer in your city, state or in the country.

- earned a new accredited designation within your industry.

- are donating several hours a week to helping the underprivileged learn how to set up a basic financial plan.

You can either act as your own publicist or hire a professional writer or agency to do it for you. If you choose the former, follow our guidelines, attend a publicity seminar given by your local media, participate in a workshop at a local college or visit your local library for "how-to" books. Also, check with your network to see what is working for them and / or for recommendations on whom to hire.

Media release guidelines:

- Use 8 1/2-inch x 11-inch paper.

- Use your letterhead or plain white bond paper.

- Type copy, double spaced to leave room for editor's comments.

- In the upper left-hand corner, type "For more information, contact (your name and phone number)." If you do not use your letterhead, also type your company name, address, phone and fax numbers, and e-mail and web addresses.

- Put "For Immediate Release" and the date under the identification.

- Include the five "Ws" (who, what, when, where, why) and one "H" (how) in the first paragraph or two, whenever possible.

- Type "more" on the bottom of each page except the last, where you can put "30" or "###."

Sample Press Release

For more information, contact
Lillian D. Bjorseth, President
Duoforce Enterprises, Inc.
630-983-5308, 630-983-5312 (fax)
lillian@duoforce.com
www.duoforce.com

For Immediate Release
April 1, 2002

(Lisle IL) Lillian D. Bjorseth has created and published unique new tools that help associations, entrepreneurs and any-size businesses enhance their marketing and relationship-building prowess.

"Called *52 Ways To Break The Ice & Target Your Market*, the product is built around two decks of cards carefully crafted to make ordinary encounters extraordinary, Bjorseth said.

"The 26 **ICE BREAKERS** can be used whenever two or more people gather. They help you overcome your natural hesitancy to talk with people you know only fleetingly or even people you see regularly," Bjorseth said. "They make networking and word-of-mouth marketing easier for everyone, and, especially, for over half of the population who is introverted. They help people get past business-card exchanges to business-building exchanges," she added.

more

The 26 **MARKET TARGETERS** help associations, large and small companies, as well as people seeking jobs, brainstorm and refine marketing information and strategies. "They help you hone your efforts to let the world know you are unique and have built a better mousetrap," Bjorseth said.

An instructional manual shows you how to use the cards, provides user and venue possibilities and gives you suggestions to enhance the use of the **MARKET TARGETERS.**

Bjorseth has decades of experience as a communication and networking skills trainer, speaker and consultant. She coached top executives at AT&T in media and communication skills before starting Duoforce Enterprises, Inc. 12 years ago.

She is also author of *Breakthrough Networking: Building Relationships That Last,* the *Nothing Happens Until We Communicate* audiotape and workbook series and a contributing author to *Masters of Networking.*

She's a member of the National Speakers Association, the National Association of Women Business Owners, the Naperville Chamber of Commerce and an adjunct professor for the Lewis University Graduate School of Management and a member of its MBA Executive Advisory Board.
The product can be ordered at www.duoforce.com or 630-983-5308.

#

Adapt these guidelines to your screen when you e-mail releases.

Five Ws and One H

Using the previous press release, here are the five Ws and one H:

- ◆ Who: Lillian D. Bjorseth, president of Duoforce Enterprises, Inc.

- ◆ What: Created new product, *52 Ways To Break The Ice & Target Your Market*

- ◆ When: Now; new product

- ◆ Where: Lisle IL

- ◆ Why: To help associations, entrepreneurs and businesses enhance their marketing and relationship-building abilities

- ◆ How: Through two special decks of cards and an instructional manual

Helpful hint: Some of you may find it easier to articulate the 5 Ws and one H before writing the release … this is like formulating the topic sentence before starting to write a paragraph. It helps you focus on your main message.

Where to Send Media Releases

Writing the press release is only half the job; deciding whom to send it to can take just as long or even longer. Begin by checking your local phone directory for newspapers, magazines and radio and television stations that cover your area—if the news is local. For regional or national releases, expand your search. The library is a great source for state and national media directories and also is helpful in ascertaining if directories are web-based or not. Check the web for online opportunities.

Who to send the release to at a newspaper, radio or television station is another important consideration. Larger papers have many editors, such as book, business, education, entertainment, food and real estate. Zero in on the person who is interested in your subject area. One of the surest ways to have your efforts go for naught is to send information to the wrong editor or a publication that does not deal with your subject matter. If you are in doubt, review several issues of the publication online or at the library, buy an issue at a newsstand, subscribe to the publication or call for a preview copy.

Many media experts suggest you send a release to a person's name rather than to "business editor," for example. While this may be the preferred way, it does have drawbacks. The major one is the time and effort needed to keep your database current.

Media personnel change assignments frequently. If you have 30 to 50 media on your list, you can spend an inordinate amount of time keeping your list up-to-date. At a minimum, though, you need to know your local contacts by name.

For any special event or announcement, follow up with a phone call within a week to make sure your material has been received and to answer any questions the editor may have. This also provides you a good opportunity to reaffirm a name, establish rapport with the person, let them know you are more than a name on a press release, or stay in touch if you have already built a relationship.

I used to think reporters and editors didn't want to be bothered (and some don't!); however, a news anchor at a major Chicago radio station assured me he pays more attention to those who follow up.

Don't be disappointed if your release doesn't appear right away, especially if the information is not date dependent. Editors often save information until they have a special need or are low on news.

Also, your releases—whether used or not—may help to establish you as a subject matter expert (SME) in your field.

One day you may get an unexpected call from a reporter when he/she needs a response to a national or regional "happening" in your field of expertise.

Also, your releases ... may help to establish you as a subject matter expert (SME) in your field.

Another shock for people new at the publicity game is that their phone doesn't ring off the hook even when the news makes the paper or your interview airs. Readers must need your product or service to call you immediately. Many people file the information for when they may need it.

> *When my friend and I started a singles organization, we received a lot of newspaper coverage, including a full-page feature story. Even though the group disbanded after six months (it worked quickly for me!), I received phone calls about the organization for at least another six months from people who had clipped newspaper articles. One woman told me she had been "involved" at the time and put it aside in case she found herself unattached again. She was!*

If your press release is the spark for a feature story (an in-depth article about you or your business written by newspaper staff), get permission from the paper to reprint it. Then turn it into a marketing tool and send it to customers and prospects. It's a great way to let others know about your business and can also be a refresher for clients you haven't talked to for a while. If you appear on electronic media, you can ask for a tape.

It's part of what I call the "ripple effect." Just as a stone continues to create waves when you throw it into the water, so should your publicity keep creating more and more recognition for you. Publicize the fact in other media, such as organizational and professional association newsletters, that you were featured in print or electronically.

It's part of what I call the "ripple effect."

Publicity is part of your networking program and, as such, is part of your image-building plan for you and / or your company. When people see your name again and again in the media, they begin to think you are for real; therefore, getting media attention will speed up your name recognition and your business and career success.

chapter 18

The Effect of
Gender Differences

Opposites may attract in romance; in business, likes prefer to deal with likes. This has been more of a relationship-building plus for men and more of a drawback for women. Things are changing, but the situation still favors men since almost all the Fortune 500 companies are run by men and male-dominated boards of directors. The old boy network is alive in the office and on the golf course, where men long have successfully conducted business. Fortunately, more and more women are learning to intertwine sales with their chip shots.

**Fortunately, more and more women
are learning to intertwine sales with
their chip shots.**

Self-employed women (and this might be why their numbers are increasing daily) have an immediate advantage: As owners and presidents, they start, title-wise, on an equal basis with men. They have power. They have control.

Sometimes, titles are not enough. Call it male bonding, the old boy network or whatever you wish—men still subtly band together through the topics they choose to discuss or ignore. Since men are still the power brokers and set the business pace, they still have a strong say about what is and is not okay to talk about. Having good social rapport enhances business relationships, so being left out of a conversation can also mean being left out when the contracts are let.

Men Talk to Inform; Women Talk to Relate

Differences in communication styles contribute to this freeze out. The major difference—and a block—to successful communication across genders is why men and women talk.

Men talk to inform, so they generally communicate in a straightforward way and get to the point quickly.

Susan asks Bill: "Should I attend our chamber of commerce after-hours event?"

Bill: "Yes. Businesspeople invite you as a guest into their office or store to network with 50 to 100 other people. You meet a lot of potential customers."

Now, let's reverse the situation.

Bill asks Susan: "Should I attend our chamber's after-hours event?"

Susan: "Oh, yes, absolutely! Members invite you into their business place. You see how they decorate and who else works there. I remember going to a real estate agency. Would you believe they all sat in one big room? Imagine all those people selling simultaneously!"

Bill: "Hmmm."

Susan: "It's a great networking opportunity. So many business people show up. I met a dozen new people the last time."

Bill: "Maybe, I'll go. I'll think about it."

Susan: "Think about it? How can you not go?"

Women connect and bond through talking. They strive to understand others better and to improve relationships. They are, or at least appear to be, more interested in people and their feelings. This often leads to an indirect approach that men may see as unsure or lacking confidence. Susan gave Bill far more information than he wanted or needed to make a decision. She wanted to convince him and thought that the more she said about the people and surroundings, the more credible her argument would be. Instead, women often say "too much," according to men.

At one of my workshops for insurance agents (all male), one of them said, "It often takes women so long to answer my questions that I forget what I asked!"

Even I as a woman thought Alicia went too far when she called for information about my former leads group and soon was telling me that her sister's husband's father had passed away at the same time her sister's daughter was in the hospital recovering from bulimia.

Women tend to disclose personal information and expect the same from others; they may feel personally rejected if others don't follow suit. Men like to give their opinions about sports and politics but prefer not to disclose information about their personal life. At a business event, they do not ask these questions of others, either.

> *As Allison joined a group of men and I who were chatting before a dinner meeting, she said, "I'm so glad to be here. My husband is out of town, my first sitter canceled and, at the last minute, I got one of the neighbors to do me a favor." The conversation came to an abrupt halt. After a short silence, the men continued talking about Sunday's football game.*
>
> *Allison told me later that she felt momentarily rejected and disappointed she had tried so hard to make the meeting. She soon felt better, though, as we wove her into the conversation, she said.*

It was nothing personal. Before Allison joined the group, none of the men had mentioned word one about marital status or family. They had been having an animated discussion about a recent football game. She had put them on the spot, and they chose to stay in their comfort zone.

Men and women would both benefit from compromise. Men can learn to be comfortable with more subjects like wellness and fitness, general-interest topics like books, magazines, movies and the theater; and women can bone up on sports and current events.

Read the newspaper and/or listen to television or news reports the day you will be attending a networking event. Listen to the car radio on your way there. Be aware of what has gone on so you can meaningfully contribute to a conversation. Further, analyze what has happened, form opinions and then offer them. People don't need to agree with one another to enjoy sharing a conversation. In fact, you can benefit and grow from hearing divergent viewpoints.

Women, Learn to Be More Direct

When communicating with men or in mixed company, women can improve their relationship-building success and be perceived as more powerful when they follow these five easy steps:

1. Use Declarative Sentences

Unless you specifically need to get someone's approval or consent, speak in declarative rather than interrogatory sentences. Women tend to take the question-asking process a step too far with tag questions.

It's a good sales promotional item, isn't it?

The sentence was fine—until the last two words.

Since women generally are reared to please rather than be pleased, this need for approval is a carryover from childhood when we wanted that consent from our parents and our peers. I remember going shopping with my girlfriends and finding a scarf or blouse I liked. Then, I would say:

"This is a nice scarf, isn't it?

If one of them said, "No," I wouldn't think of buying it. I was dependent on their approval. This doesn't mean you can't ask questions. Simply eliminate the "tag" at the end.

"Do you like this scarf?"

"Do you agree it's a good sales promotional item?"

Learn to make up your own mind and approve of yourself. This will help you automatically eliminate tag questions and ask questions authoritatively when you choose the interrogatory mode.

2. Use the Active Voice

The active voice shows ownership, and it puts you on a limb. It means you take responsibility for your actions, which, of course, also means you are willing to take the consequences ... and accept the rewards. You are in charge!

> *Active voice: "The people in my department and I voted 'no' to the company's suggestion that we consider flex hours."*

> *Passive voice: "It has been decided by the people in my department and I that we would rather not have flex hours."*

Both convey the same message; however, the tone is entirely different. One speaks authoritatively; the other is far less so.

3. Eliminate Weak Words

Speak with conviction! When you want to set up a meeting with a prospect, say so:

> *Strong: "I'd like to take you to lunch and discuss the program further."*

> *Weak: "I don't know what a good time is for you, of if you even want to, but we could have lunch to discuss the program further."*

Words that can make you a weak communicator include:

- ◆ Dumb
- ◆ Just
- ◆ Little
- ◆ Moment
- ◆ Only

Never preface a question with: "This may be a dumb question, but ..." Many people associate "dumb" with the person asking the question. Why demean yourself with the first words out of your mouth? Is your purpose to ask a question or to tell people you have nothing important to say? Don't be surprised if you are ignored—then and at future meetings.

No need to apologize. If you want to know the answer, ask the question and leave out the "dumb." Make sure, for your credibility, that you have been listening and that the information has not already been given.

While "I just want a little (a moment) of your time," is the active voice, it still connotes a lack of confidence on your part. In fact, you indicate you are not even sure you should be asking to meet with the person and that he/she will be doing you a favor.

Approach the person as an equal—your time is valuable, too—tell them you need to meet with them and find out what time/day is good.

> *"I want to set up a meeting with you. Is 10 AM Thursday okay?"*

Administrative assistants and medical office personal often use weak words when trying to get on their boss's calendar. Demand through your actions to be treated as a professional. You can respect advanced degrees without undermining yourself as an individual.

You can respect advanced degrees without undermining yourself as an individual.

---

4. Maximize the Impact of Your Words

Say what you mean, and mean what you say.

> *"I have a referral for you. John is looking for a top-notch graphic designer."*

rather than

"This may not work out, but I'll give you John's card anyway since he is looking for a graphic designer. Hopefully, you can connect."

Another way women minimize the importance of what they say is to speak in a hesitant manner, which leads to the last point.

5. Don't Hedge

"I'm not sure how you wanted to proceed, so here are three ideas for you to consider."

There are times we need to give people options; other times, we use them to avoid making a decision. Deborah Tannen, in her book *That's Not What I Meant*, says women often use these kinds of tactics so that when they meet with a negative response, they can say, "That's not what I meant." Then they can change their mind and make new recommendations. (12)

We discussed earlier the importance of condensing your verbal business card into a few sentences and being comfortable with it. Do the same type of preparation for meetings and networking events. Know your purpose and your main message or reason for attending. This will enable you to get your points across quickly and effectively.

Importance of Listening

One of your most important communication skills is listening. It is the most used (the average person spends about 45 percent of the day listening), yet the least taught. Few people have had more than a few days or a week of intensive listening training.

The lack of training becomes even more acute when you add to it the fact that men and women listen differently. Let's look at the process first. It is hierarchical, meaning that each step depends on the one before it, and they must be done in order.

1. Sensing

Hearing is the first step and is the physiological process that happens when your ears hear sound waves. Some people—both men and women—never seem to move beyond this step!

Sensing, even though it is a passive step, is basic to the other activities. You must hear the message before you can act upon it.

2. Interpreting

This second step is the one that leads to understanding and misunderstanding.

To understand this step better, think of human beings as having a giant filtering system. Everything you hear passes

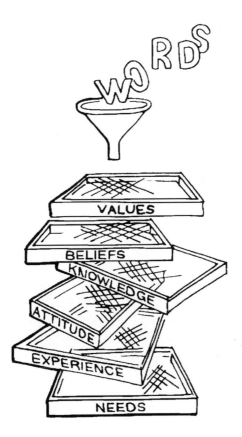

through that system, which is made up of your needs, values, beliefs, knowledge, attitudes and experiences. The challenge in the communication process is to assign the meaning to the words that the speaker intended—not the ones that fit your own needs.

You clean your car and furnace filters so they will function more efficiently—do the same with your internal filtering system so you can more efficiently process the tremendous amount of information that bombards you daily.

Cleaning your system means getting rid of preconceived notions and prejudices, anger, selfishness and self-centered attitudes so you can listen to others with an open mind.

3. Evaluating

In this step, you weigh the information, sort fact from opinion and make judgments—to decide whether to agree or disagree with the speaker. Again, we compare what is being said to our storehouse of knowledge gleaned from experience.

The danger is when you begin this activity too soon and tune out the speaker the minute you hear something you don't agree with or that doesn't mesh with stored information.

If you start to prepare your comeback before the speaker finishes (depending on how emotional the issue is, you may get agitated before your turn comes), you stop sensing and interpreting and thwart the listening process. You also may miss vital information you need to assess before you respond.

4. Understanding

You owe it to the speaker to try to comprehend accurately the meaning and significance of what is being said. Taking the time to understand other people's opinions or how they interpret information does not mean you have to accept their way of thinking as your own. It simply means you give them the right to express themselves.

5. Responding

In this step, you let the speaker know if he/she is getting through. Reactions can be verbal (asking questions, agreeing, stating your opinions) or nonverbal (smiling, frowning, nodding, folding your arms). This is the first point where you help speakers see if they are getting through, i.e., if their message is being heard.

6. Remembering

Once you have received and acted on the message, you must store it for future use. Studies have shown that 75 percent of what you hear passes right through. You may retain as much as 50 percent for 48 hours; however, after that, the average retention level drops to 25 percent.

Add this factor to the gender differences we will discuss next, and you begin to see the need to sharpen your listening skills to build better relationships that last!

How Men and Women Differ ...

Listening is a participatory sport; it involves active and passive interpersonal skills. Women make more direct eye contact and smile more when they are listening, which, in turn, often leads to mixed messages. (Men may accept the pleasant demeanor as acceptance or agreement while women may merely be listening politely.) When they are speaking, however, women often avert direct eye contact, looking over their audiences or down at the table or floor.

Men make direct eye contact when they are speaking and let their eyes wander more when they are listening, which often makes women think they are not paying attention.

When I was training two new male leaders to head a chapter of my former leads group, I was amazed how well one of them personified this principle! He looked at his co-leader and me when he spoke. When I spoke, he either was racing ahead in his kit or shuffling materials on his desk. Several times, he closed the kit, waited a minute, opened it and seemed to be trying to follow me. Once, he even excused himself and left the office for a few minutes!

I so much wanted to give him a test on what I had just said since I knew he was missing so much of what I was sharing.

The other man more than made up for his deficiencies. He periodically looked at me, and more importantly, was following along right down to the letter.

Sadly, I was correct. The first man I referred to had not listened, failed to handle his responsibilities and eventually had to be removed as a leader.

At home, men may be reading the newspaper, listening to a ball game on the radio, watching another one on television and still tell the women in their life that they are listening! Which leads us to another difference: Women are much better at reading nonverbals and integrating them with the verbals to understand what the speaker is really "saying." (Remember from Chapter 7 that 93 percent of what we communicate is in how we say it, not what we say.)

When men are involved with the newspaper, radio and television simultaneously, they miss a woman's body language (55 percent) since they are not looking at her—and maybe some of the vocal and verbal communication message as well. The woman is correct when she says, "He's not listening to me."

Another difference is "listening noises." Women use words like "hmmm," "uh-huh" and "okay" to let the other person know they are keeping up with the conversation. This is exactly what women mean by these "noises." They are hearing what others are saying, not necessarily agreeing with what is being said. Men, who listen quietly, accept these sounds as concurrence, which leads to miscommunication at the office and at home.

Both sexes need to become more aware in cross-gender conversations.

Women: Say what you mean emphatically as you look 'em in the eye. Get rid of listening noises.

Men: Listen with your eyes and ears and learn to read body language better.

Women and men: Read a book on improving listening skills and/or take a listening course. When in doubt, always listen more than you speak.

"God gave us two ears and one mouth so we could listen twice as much as we talk."—Folk Saying

chapter **19**

The Role in Keeping/ Changing Jobs

Knowing how to network professionally gives you more control over your career! It gives you an edge in moving laterally or being promoted within your company, finding new positions on the outside, and in being positioned well should your company downsize, right size or reengineer you out of a job.

With "job security" becoming passé in today's business climate, networking is no longer optional, even if you are gainfully employed. And, when you find a new job, chances are good that you may move again, and again, and again before you retire. After your mandatory retirement age, you may find yourself still needing additional income to pay the bills or to live in the manner you have chosen.

It's a given that you need to be good at what you do. Integrity and good character also help. Networking won't work if you choose not to start from a solid foundation. It may open doors for you; however, you may never be welcomed inside or ask to remain for any length of time if you don't perform up to the company's or your supervisor's standards.

Before we examine the "how-tos," let's look at the benefits of personal recommendations and the face-to-face meetings they can lead to.

Value of Networking in Job Searches

- ◆ It's a door opener.
- ◆ 80 to 90 percent of jobs are never listed publicly.
- ◆ Success rates increase dramatically with personal references.
- ◆ It is easier to overcome objections in person.
- ◆ A position may be created or modified just for you.
- ◆ Negotiations can be swayed in your favor.
- ◆ Interviewers may give you job leads and entrees to other internal and external jobs.

Let People Know You Exist—Within Your Company

The following relationship-building suggestions make you more visible at your place of employment and set the stage for lateral moves and promotions.

1. Participate in Service Projects
Offer your services for the United Way campaign, the Red Cross blood drive, savings bonds drives. Choose projects you enjoy and believe in and that will show others you care. These

projects typically are headed by a top company official and also involve other company directors and managers. If your director is involved, offer to handle details for him/her. You'll have a chance to work with peers from other departments and get recognition while contributing to worthwhile causes. Incidentally, it probably will also increase your outside exposure.

> *One of my assignments at AT&T Bell Laboratories was coordinating the United Way campaign for one of its locations. Because the emphasis was on providing information rather than on "strongly suggesting" employees give a certain percent like many other Bell companies did at the time, it was a giant undertaking. I spent many weekend and nighttime hours on the project.*
>
> *The heads of the campaign both years I worked on it were the location's ranking officers, one of whom later started AT&T's computer systems division after divestiture in 1984. Because of our prior acquaintance through United Way, I was asked to help spearhead public relations for the venture, a position that gained me international exposure.*

2. Eat in the Cafeteria

This provides a good opportunity to be seen by everyone in the company! Politics vary within companies, but at one gas utility where I worked, it was considered obligatory. The chairman always ate there when he was in town, and he liked others to do the same. As an aside, he always wore his suit jacket to the cafeteria. All the men—and some of the women—did, too!

Lunchtime can be a good opportunity to get to know people better. Conversations often drift to non-business subjects. Listen more than you talk, and you will learn a lot more. If company policy is to eat with people from your own department, do so—most of the time. When meetings you are attending break for lunch, use the time to eat with other attendees. Frequently, it's an opportunity to rub elbows with higher ups.

3. Offer Positive Suggestions

Let management know positive ways it can enhance production and improve the bottom line. Some companies have an official suggestion box. If not, make sure your ideas eventually reach the top through appropriate channels. Additionally, you may be written up in the company newsletter or be recognized on bulletin boards or through company-wide notices in print or through e-mail.

4. Take Part in Company Functions

While functions vary by company—outings, dinner dances, family picnics —they frequently are "pet projects" of management, who keep mental records of who attends. Other times, they are just fun ways of getting your family to meet other families (all of whom have networks). They give you a chance to meet co-workers on a less formal basis—with their hair down—and, again, help you get to know another side of them. You may discover you share a favorite hobby or sport and find a new basis on which to build and strengthen your relationship.

Find out immediately what your company's unwritten attendance policy is on after-hour functions. Supervisors often are privy to information that can help you; however, it may be so commonplace to them that they forget to mention it. Don't knowingly hurt your future chances by *not* attending. If you have corporate experience, you already know the importance of "unwritten" rules!

Politics may be less rigidly adhered to outside the office, and it may be all right for you to talk at length with people several levels above you—in the office, you might be crucified for attempting it. Position yourself near someone you want to speak with, and it will be more natural for him/her to pull you into the conversation or for you to slip in.

Be pleasant and friendly to everyone there. No exceptions! Everyone is worth smiling at and speaking with. Dress and act professionally. "After-hours" or "off-premises" is not an excuse for low-cut tops, short skirts, T-shirts with offensive sayings or off-color jokes. Others will remember on Monday morning.

Or you may choose to participate in company-sponsored sports teams or other after-hour employee-only events. They frequently are less political, give you the option to get to know people better over a longer period of time and have the side benefit of being a healthy activity. One of the positive things is that all of you already have a commonality: You enjoy the sport or activity enough to want to voluntarily be involved in it.

5. Get Your Name in Print

People need to see your name repeatedly to keep it inscribed in their minds. One vehicle for wide publicity is your company's newsletter. First of all, get to know the editor. Volunteer to be a reporter for your department and submit news items on a regular basis. Offer to write an article in your area of expertise. Make photo suggestions. Write a letter to the editor.

Inform the editors of awards/honors/recognition you (and others in your department) have received outside your company, i.e., from professional/civic/social organizations.

Special events call for committees, and committees often print fliers that list who to contact. The fliers are posted on bulletin boards for weeks and even months. Make sure you share in this free opportunity for publicity, while contributing to your company.

6. Be Creative

Look for ways to publicize yourself and your activities— discreetly and professionally.

- ◆ Participate in special events like Black History and Women's History Months, Asian-American Week, Cinco de Mayo programs.

- ◆ Have a booth at a noon-time hobby show sponsored by the company.

- ◆ Help plan and run holiday events for employees and their families.

Let People Know You Exist — Outside Your Company

Now, let's look at ways to increase your visibility outside your company.

1. Join Organizations/Clubs

Reread Chapter 11 to refresh your memory on how to decide what to join and how to get the most benefits. Additionally, answer these questions. Do I want to:

- ◆ Meet peers from other local companies?

- ◆ Move geographically and, therefore, scope out the market in other parts of the country?

- ◆ Become an officer in the organization?

- ◆ Present programs/train within the organization?

- ◆ Establish more credibility in my field through membership?

- ◆ Grow professionally through the group?

- ◆ Change jobs?

  Early in my career when I was employed in public relations, I joined an area press association to establish better relations with the local press. Little did I know that the networking I was to do would lead to my next two jobs!

When I decided to go back to full-time employment after several years of freelancing, I called the director of public relations for a gas utility and asked if he would circulate my resumés among his contacts. The day my resumé landed on his desk, one of his employees quit. I received an immediate call, and two weeks later I was on his staff.

Two years later when I wanted to move on, I called a contact at what was then Illinois Bell. Since I wanted to work in Chicago's western suburbs, he advised me to call the public relations manager at AT&T Bell Labs near my home. It so happened that out of 2,700 employees, he had two public relations professionals on his staff, and one had just left. He asked for my resumé and assured me he would not circulate it to others. He wanted to interview me. I got the job!

Networking works!

2. Attend Trade Shows

Attend those within your industry if you want to get your name known by your competitors. Move outside your industry when your goal is to switch fields. (The clearer you are about your goals, the more quickly you can build relationships to accomplish your purpose.) Major players have booths; smaller companies send representatives to walk the floors, attend the workshops and network. The workshops, by the way, are an easy way to get more information about industry trends and priorities. (Offer to present a workshop, if you have the expertise and inclination. The publicity can do wonders for you!)

Hang around the hall, talk to meeting participants and get yourself invited to the after-hour receptions where top management shows up. Attendees have time to chat; they are away from the day-to-day grind and are happy to answer questions about their company and share industry insights. Offer to take people to lunch or dinner. If your company pays your way fine; if not, it may be worth your while to use some of your frequent flier miles and your own money to attend. You will meet the movers and shakers and hear the industry's prognosis for the next six months or even six years. Keynote speakers are typically visionaries for the industry.

3. Attend Conferences and Workshops

Your choices can vary from industry conferences to professional development workshops. In addition to increasing your knowledge, you will again have the opportunity to mingle with people from many other businesses and environments. Use the breaks to get to know them better.

Turn your cell phone off. Leave your laptop at the office. You can handle routine affairs when you get back. The task at hand is by far the most important in the moment.

4. Attend After-Hour Networking Events

These activities, which may be sponsored by groups you belong to or independents, may take only an extra hour out of your day and can contribute immensely to your career. Stop by, be seen, and shake a few hands. Doing it on a regular basis will increase your visibility and the possibility that people will choose you to do business with, to recommend for a job opening or an interview.

A common thread running through the preceding suggestions is to get to know others. When they have an opening or hear of one, *you* may have the talents, abilities and presentation skills they want. Make sure yours is the first name that comes to mind, i.e., gain top-of-the-mind positioning. First, though, they need to know you exist!

Know What Is Going On!

Just as you must be known, you must also know what is happening.

1. Develop a Grapevine

It's the one way to know what is *really* happening and why it happened. Good grapevines are built on trust and integrity. I have a simple rule: To see if you can trust someone, tell something to only that person. If the information gets out, you have your answer. If it doesn't, you also have your answer.

Good grapevines are built on trust and integrity.

Beware of rumormongers! They tend to destroy themselves. Make sure they don't take you down with them.

Grapevines are *the* source to find out about internal and external job openings before they become public knowledge (80 to 90 percent of all job openings are not officially advertised). Internally, use your contacts to find out what the supervision is like, the climate of the department, if the job is wired, amount of travel involved and other details relevant to you.

Externally, stay in touch with your contacts. Call them. Take them to lunch. Above all, make sure you can trust them when a job change is your goal. Woe for you should the news prematurely get back to your management.

Always be discreet and professional. Bad news travels faster than good. Don't let a careless rumor permanently hurt you.

2. Read, Read, Read

Start with your company's newsletters, policy statements and annual reports. Include industry and general publications. Make the newspaper a daily habit. (If you are short on time, catch the headlines on radio, television or the Internet.) Be and stay informed.

Become an expert on your company and on your competition. If you wish to move from Madison Avenue to Wall Street, switch your concentration from advertising publications to financial.

How To Use Networking To Job Hunt

Your business and personal associates can become your greatest allies when you are changing jobs, either by choice or because someone else chose for you.

1. Prepare Verbal Business Card

The introduction we discussed in Chapter 12 is a good place to start. When you are networking for a job or job change, you may wish to hone it slightly for different situations. Practice until you feel comfortable with all your variations. You may have to emphasize aspects of your career that you did not normally talk about before you were job-seeking. Don't say "I'm in transition" in the first few sentences.

2. Develop Job Wish List

Know what you are seeking so you know when you have found it! Use the following form to help you.

My Job-Hunting Plan

Kind of Job	Company/ Industry	Salary Desired: (will settle for)	Preferred Location	Status
Marketing manager	Graphic design	$75,000 ($65,000)	Chicago area	

3. Research Job Market

This is a vital step that many people overlook or purposely pass up because "it's boring!" If you choose to do it yourself:

◆ Browse company websites.

◆ Keep your ears tuned for mergers/acquisitions/takeovers.

◆ Read newspapers, magazines, newsletters.

◆ Talk to people in the industry.

◆ Visit the library.

If you want professional help:

◆ Find a good executive recruiter.

◆ Hire someone to do the research.

◆ Use an outplacement/career counseling firm.

Know the trends and economic forecasts for the industries you have chosen. If your first choice is in a declining industry, rethink your decision. Check the emerging industries. Do any of them interest you? Could you swap your diminished enthusiasm for job security? What is most important to you? Is it time to go it alone?

4. Network With Others in Transition

If you are part of a corporate downsizing, you already have co-workers with whom to brainstorm and communicate, and you may be sharing the same outplacement services. Even then, you may wish to expand your network quickly and find people in other disciplines and industries for mutual help and support. This is especially important if you feel alone and/or lonely in your search. Don't rely on your family to fill this important need. Find someone else to share with how badly the interview may have gone rather than making it dinnertime conversation. Keep focusing on the positive in your personal life.

Options for building relationships with others in your same situations include:

- Career and job centers

- Career coaches

- Church and synagogue-organized groups

- Independently run organizations for people in transition (There are a plethora of these in the Chicago area.)

- Outplacement firms

Benefits vary according to your needs, and they include:

- Expanded job search options

- Likelihood of meeting people who understand and empathize with your plight

- Planned regular activities/events to attend

- Programs to improve your communication/ networking/resumé-writing skills

- Opportunity to interact with people not emotionally/ financially dependent on you

- Reason to get out of bed

- Valuable feedback on your approach, your image and your materials

5. Make Contact List

Be realistic! Include anyone you think can help you. However, make sure they are people you have built relationships with so they will be comfortable—and willing—to help you. If you choose to include someone you have not spoken to for years, suggest getting together and renewing the acquaintance before you ask for help.

My Contact List

Who I Know	Phone #	Whom They Know	Status	Date

If you haven't stayed in touch with people, they may be hesitant to refer you to others, and with good reason! They don't know if you were right sized, downsized or ostracized, which is where they may find themselves if they refer you without first checking the facts. This is another good reason for you to build and maintain relationships throughout your career!

Make the list as complete as possible. The more information you include, the more helpful you will find it. Keep updating the list, even when you find another job. It can be a valuable tool throughout the rest of your career.

When you have listed all your contacts, add the following information:

- Put a check mark (√) by those you feel comfortable calling.

- Put an (x) by those you want to send a letter.

- Put an (*) by those you know but want someone else to talk with first.

6. Prepare Package of Materials

Put together a sampling of your materials to sell yourself to a prospective employer or to sell someone on recommending you for an interview. Contents will vary according to your background and experience but will include the following:

- Resumé (a must!)

- Samples of your work/photos of actual projects

- Bylined articles written by you

- Newspaper or magazine articles written about you

- Testimonials/letters of endorsement

Prepare extra copies of your package so you will always have one available. It's a good idea to keep several in your briefcase, and even in your car, should you unexpectedly meet a prospect.

If you cannot get enough originals for your package, i.e., the newsletter you wrote for a client, get permission to make copies. Use at least a 60-lb. stock for reproduction. First impressions are crucial.

7. Prepare for the Interview

Getting the interview is the first step. You still have important work to do before your appointment. You need to prepare personally and professionally to make the best impression. Reread Chapters 6 and 7 on the important roles appearance and behavior play in the nonverbal messages you give. (Meet with an image consultant, if necessary.) Also, you need to research the company.

First, visit the company's website. Then, ask someone at the company to send you brochures, annual reports or other relevant literature you can review ahead of time. Be familiar with the company's revenues, sales, number of employees, number of locations (what is the size and function of the one you will be visiting?), founding date and officer information.

If the company is a nonprofit association, get a piece of stationery that usually lists the board of directors. These people are important corporate and community leaders. Do you know any of them? Do you know anyone who knows one of them or works for one of them? If so, solicit information from them. Can you get a personal endorsement?

Use the information as background. Don't flaunt it or begin to cite statistics. The interviewer knows how many employees the company has and who the president is!

If you have doubts about the preparation process, consult a career consultant. Many of them offer you an options package and allow you to pick and choose areas where you want assistance.

8. Write Thank-You Letters

Take the time to say "thank you" to everyone who helps you—no matter how small the effort. Also, keep people up-to-date on leads they have given you. You will find people more willing to continue to assist when you take time to show appreciation. Make thank-you notes a part of your office supplies. Use waiting times in offices and airports to get the notes out on a timely basis.

Also, write to the person who interviewed you. This one should be typewritten if sent in the mail ... or a formal e-mail. Keep it short (unless you promised to send additional information) and upbeat. It won't guarantee you the job; however, it will show consideration.

9. Ask for Feedback

To improve and be the best you can be, you need feedback. Ask for it from a prospective employer, if appropriate. Family, friends and professional associates can critique your materials and image. Ask them to be frank. Accept their comments as constructive criticism.

Keep a positive attitude. You will never get the "perfect" job until you feel you are "perfect" for the job.

chapter 20

On the Road

Overnight travel is an accepted part of doing business. Trips range from one-nighters to multi-day excursions. Either way, time spent away from the office can be used to stay in touch or to broaden your network across state and country boundaries. These contacts can be as valuable as those in your own city, or you may even make more contacts from your own backyard.

Jean struck up a conversation with the woman seated next to her on a flight from Chicago to New York. It turned out both were on their way to attend a national meeting of the professional communicators' organization they belonged to in Chicago, yet they had never met at a local meeting. Since, the two have frequently had lunch and shared marketing and other business advice.

Another benefit is that people you meet from other cities often have business contacts, friends or family in your city and are delighted to connect the two of you. Make a good impression, and you can almost be ensured of an introduction.

Planning business get-togethers also can be an alternative to having dinner alone or spending the evening in your room. No matter how progressive society may have become, some people still look askance at a woman having a drink alone, even if she is still wearing her business suit from the day's activities.

To make the most productive use of your time away from the office, follow these general guidelines.

Keep a Business/Networking Kit Packed

Last-minute details at the office and personal packing often occupy the hours before you leave. Do what you can ahead of time to make the trip productive. Keeping a kit packed will ensure that you have the tools necessary to build and cement relationships in the air and on the ground. Necessary ingredients include:

◆ Business cards

◆ Company/personal stationery

◆ Pens/pencils

◆ Personal address book

◆ Stamps

Items that must be taken at the last minute from your office include:

◆ Business address book

◆ Calendar/date book

◆ Clippings, articles you want to send to others

◆ Electronic hand-held devices

♦ Laptop computer

♦ Reading materials

Be sure to refill the kit as soon as you get home so it will be ready for your next trip.

Do Your Homework

Don't wait until you get to Columbus or Los Angeles to make your plans. Do your homework days and weeks ahead.

1. Use Your Network

Mention your travel plans to friends, family and associates who might know someone or know about a professional organization or event in the city you will be visiting. Read the networking section of industry/professional magazines for upcoming events throughout the country.

Scan your business cards for anyone you have met and your list from Chapter 11 for anyone you would like to meet in that city. Call ahead to schedule an appointment. If your days already are full, ask the other person if it would be okay to meet for a short time before or after work. Offer to buy him/her breakfast or dinner if you really want the meeting.

2. Check Organizational Directories

Civic groups, such as Rotary and Lions, have chapters throughout the country and can be a great way for you to meet people with whom you share a common interest. Organizations such as the National Association of Female Executives (headquartered in New York) have networking groups throughout the country and will gladly share directors' names with members. Use professional membership directories in the same way, i.e., the Public Relations Society of America has chapters in all major cities.

3. Be Ready With Small Talk

Be prepared to start conversations and to hold your own with people you meet in a limousine or taxi, in the airport area and on the plane. Listen to the radio, and read the newspaper before departing to get an overview of the "hot news" for the day. The limo company that I use has a daily newspaper waiting for me.

Swing Into Action When You Arrive

If you are attending a conference or meeting that has a get-acquainted event the night before, go to it. You are likely to meet other people who have come solo, and you will have something in common to talk about immediately. You may find another person or a group with whom to have dinner.

If you enjoy working out, choose a hotel with a health club. If circumstances are right, strike up a conversation and you may find a dinner partner since most people work out before eating.

I arrived the evening before for a business conference and immediately used the hotel's workout facilities. Another woman joined me shortly. She was from another country and there for the same meeting. We struck up a conversation, and we arranged to meet for breakfast the next day.

Ask the concierge if the hotel has any planned activities or if he/she can help you locate a specific restaurant or facility.

I am an avid Chicago Bears fan and wanted company to watch a Monday night game while out of town. The concierge directed me to another hotel with a large screen and an indoor tailgate party. It was a lot of fun, and I met other Bears fans. It beat cheering them on alone!

When you arrive at your destination, call contacts to verify your plans. If you have not yet done so, make initial contacts from your prepared list. If you need local help, check the white and Yellow Pages of the phone directory for association or organizational information or ask the concierge.

Use/Plan for Private Time

Some people look at time away from the office as private or quiet time. If that is your goal, tell as few people as possible where you can be reached. Use the time to watch television, or to catch up on your e-mail, reading and correspondence. This is where your networking kit comes into play. Write those personal or business notes you have been putting off. The stamps you brought along will ensure that you can mail the pieces right away, rather than sticking them in your briefcase and possible oblivion.

> *I once got an overdue notice from my local electric utility even though my checkbook verified that I had paid the bill. About three months later, the envelope (without the stamp) fell out of a back pocket of my briefcase. I learned the hard way.*

Another excellent activity for your hotel room is to personalize the business cards you have received during the day, which can amount to 25 to 50 at a trade show. Date them and note the event. Then, record anything you want to remember about the person and, especially, anything you promised to give them. If you have an electronic database, enter the information immediately if you have your laptop with you, and you won't even have to carry the cards home with you! You can also send "nice to meet you" e-mails to the appropriate people. Stand out from the crowd and deliver what you promised!

**Stand out from the crowd
and deliver what you promised.**

"Private" time often happens even when you do not plan for it. No traveler is immune from weather and other flight delays. Being prepared helps you relax, knowing you are catching up on office work or leisure reading.

Follow Through and Replenish When You Return Home

As soon as possible upon your return, file the business cards if you still use a manual system or enter them in your database if not done previously. Follow up with anything you promised to send, people you promised to contact, etc. File or discard magazines, clippings and other printed materials you had time to read. Refill your travel networking kit so it's ready for your next trip.

Take time to pat yourself on the back and reflect on what you accomplished before you get caught up in the daily grind. Stay in touch with your new contacts, and you may soon find them putting you in touch with their contacts.

chapter 21

Belief in Yourself

"Whatever the mind can conceive and believe, it can achieve."—Andrew Carnegie

Y ou can read this book again and again, practice all the tenets and still not be successful if you lack one important, basic concept: faith or belief in yourself. You need to believe that you deserve to be successful, and that you can have what you want. Then as you go about building relationships to enhance your business—you *will* get what you want.

Everything starts with a thought. If you don't have the thought, you'll never have the feeling. Your feelings lead to beliefs and attitudes that affect your needs and values, which affect your goals, which, in turn, affect your thoughts. As the process becomes a positive part of your life, it leads to better

thoughts of self and others. This positive process leads to increased business success.

Negative thoughts work the same way—except they are the basis for self-defeating, downbeat feelings that can quickly do you in. It's been said that it takes 13 positive thoughts to undo the affect of 1 negative thought. At that rate, it can take all day for some people to counterbalance their negativity!

Negative Thoughts

- "I'll never get the sale."
- "They want to buy from a larger company."
- "He never answers the phone."
- "I can't get this done by Friday."
- "Nobody ever gives me referrals."
- "It costs too much."
- "I can't afford to hire anybody."

- "I'm just a secretary."
- "I gave a referral to Mary, and she's never done anything for me."
- "I don't carry any weight around here."
- "I am uncomfortable at networking events."
- "Nobody will hire me. I'm 50 years old."

We get out of life what we expect. No wonder we sometimes don't get the sale or the job or the referrals. Raise your expectations to equal your wants. Then you will get what you want as well as what you expect.

Positive Thoughts

- "The sale's in the bag."
- "I can provide the customer service they want."
- "He *will* answer the phone."
- "I have plenty of time to finish the job by Friday."
- "I'll get three referrals at the meeting today."
- "I have the money to buy everything I need."
- "I can afford to hire somebody part-time."
- "I love being a secretary. I am doing what I like."
- "When I give to anyone, I get back tenfold."
- "My boss values my input."
- "I am good at building relationships."
- "I am a talented worker who will make a contribution."

Read aloud the list of negative thoughts. Do it again. Notice how down and discouraged you feel and sound by the time you are finished. Now, read the list of positive thoughts; read it once more. Notice the difference. Stop those negative thoughts now! The following exercise will help.

Stop Negative Thoughts

Try this three-step process:

1. Close your eyes and think of a symbol—a stop sign, a fire engine with bells and whistles, a hug from that special someone—that you can call on when you want to stop negative thoughts. Envision this image again and again until it becomes clear in your mind.

2. Start to think a negative thought. Stop! "See" your image. Dwell on it. Use it to heighten awareness that you are in charge and will not let negative thoughts prevail.

3. Try it again and again until your symbol becomes second nature and can instantaneously help you stop a negative thought.

Don't give up if this doesn't work immediately. Remember how long you have been letting your negativity have free rein.

Generate Positive Thoughts as Well

Use creative visualization to help you succeed. In *Psycho-Cybernetics*, Maxwell Maltz said the mind does not know the difference between a real and an imagined event. (13) Therefore, if you imagine you do incredibly well at an interview or at a conference, your mind will use that as a guide when you actually go to the event. Your subconscious will say:

> *"We've done well at this before; therefore, we can do well again!"*

Dream of Success

> *Lie down or get comfortable in your favorite chair. Close your eyes. Imagine yourself descending a flight of*

stairs. Count down from ten to one, repeating the process as many times as necessary to feel relaxed. (You might prefer soft music in the background.)

Imagine yourself driving to an important business conference. Imagine a smile on your face and positive energy surrounding you in the car.

When you get to the event, this positive aura continues to surround you. You sign in, get your nametag and, as you enter the room, one of the organizers immediately greets you. She then introduces you to two other guests nearby.

You exchange cards. One of them is a natural networking partner for you, and you decide to meet for lunch next week. You move on to get coffee and there meet someone you know from another event. You share helpful industry information with her. The two of you exchange cards again and decide it is mutually beneficial to stay in touch.

Throughout the course of the day—during the seminars, breaks and lunch—you continue to make contacts that you can help and who can help you. (Insert personalized wants and needs here. Go for it!) Envision happening what you want to have happen! Remember you can achieve what your mind conceives and believes. See yourself leaving the event, happy and content with a day well spent! (If you want to continue the process, imagine yourself following up with luncheons and other leads you made.)

There, wasn't that easy?

Dream of success again and again. Implant success in your mind, and it will happen in your life.

In addition to creative visualization, I suggest applicable affirmations on your way to business meetings and other events:

- "I am confident."
- "I am in control."
- "I am articulate."
- "I am persuasive."
- "I wisely and fairly lead meetings."
- "I positively impact people's lives."
- "I am wonderful; I deserve to be treated well."
- "I have boundless energy."
- "I accept myself. I am enough."

Words like these can help you overcome anxiety and lack of confidence.

It's much harder to worry and panic, when you keep saying:

- "I am calm and relaxed, I am in control."
- "Calmness reigns within me and around me."
- "I am confident in all surroundings."

Be realistic. Even positive thinking will not mean a sale or a million-dollar referral every time. However, your batting average will increase drastically.

Babe Ruth struck out more times than he hit home runs, yet he is revered for the latter. One home run will score only one run when you are the solo base runner. That same hit will score four runs when the bases are loaded.

Keep your bases full by building relationships, and you will always be ready to drive in the maximum number of runs.

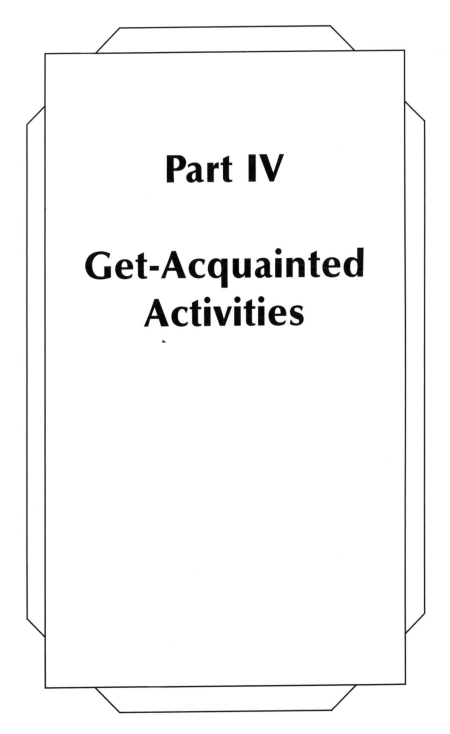

Part IV

Get-Acquainted Activities

chapter **22**

Ice Breakers

Because at least half the world is introverted, people need and appreciate help breaking the ice, i.e., starting conversations. Many are naturally hesitant to speak with strangers or people they see infrequently, like other association and group members and employees from other locations.

Whether you are sponsoring or presenting after-hours events, conferences, luncheon or dinner meetings, training sessions or workshops, one of the biggest assists you can give your participants is to start them off with a get-acquainted activity.

Participants will get into the swing of things much faster. They also will find the event more profitable and enjoyable, which means they may recommend your event or organization to others or become happier and more satisfied employees.

On the following pages, you will find a variety of ice breakers, some of them simple and easy to implement, some of them more involved—all of them guaranteed to help get people mingling and meeting. Chapter 22 consists of introductory exercises that are geared for the registration period; before a conference meal, meeting or workshop; or when there is no formal program. Chapter 23 includes exercises specifically for workshops. Suggested number of participants, materials, objective and timelines are included. Feel free to adapt to your particular audience.

52 Ways To Break The Ice & Target Your Market

Audience size: infinite

Materials: enough decks of **ICE BREAKERS** to allow one per person

Objective: to help entrepreneurs through Fortune 100 employees easily and effectively meet new people to expand their network, increase sales and enhance career success

Time: throughout registration

My experience as a business leads group owner and my years of creating and delivering training sessions and workshops prompted me to develop and publish a relationship-building product. It is built around two decks of cards. One deck of 26 **ICE BREAKERS** is crafted to help people make more meaningful and memorable interactions, especially during that crucial initial period. They encourage people to mix more quickly and effortlessly to improve communication and information flow and exchange and to increase sales and career growth opportunities. They work equally well with groups that meet regularly.

The cards provide a structured, professional and proven method to ease people's fears in a perspiration-producing situation.

Distribution methods include:

♦ Registration desk, giving one to each attendee

♦ Before event starts, by placing one on everyone's chair

♦ After everyone has been seated

♦ In conference / meeting mailing, as a teaser with a note that the card is the admission pass (Have extras on hand, just in case! And, for walk-ins.)

♦ At workshops, giving one to each participant, or by breaking up a larger group into smaller ones, each of which works on one **ICE BREAKER** collectively. An option is to have each group report back to the larger gathering.

You can find out more by visiting www.duoforce.com. An order form also is included at the end of this book.

We discuss the **MARKET TARGETERS** in more depth in Chapter 23.

Assigning Duos

Audience size: infinite

Materials: one or two baskets, business cards

Objective: to become better acquainted with one other person in a comfortable, non-threatening environment

Time: 3-5 minutes

Again, my experience with my leads group led me to develop a highly-successful process called "Duos." I have since successfully introduced the process to other groups I have headed.

The principle is simple: Two people agree to meet at a mutually convenient time like for coffee or a meal to become better acquainted with each other. The format is open; however, the goal is that both people have time to discuss their business in much more detail than is generally available during a meeting. It's also a great time to show product samples and to tap further into each other's network of 300 people.

If time allows during a meeting, people can also pair off for 5-10 minutes for more in-depth learning.

Ways to pair off:

♦ Have people put business cards into a basket, face down. Pass the basket and have everyone pick one card. The person choosing the card calls the other to set up a meeting time.

♦ Start with one person and assign him/her to meet with the person two people away. Continue in this "every-other" fashion. This works well since people frequently sit next to someone they already know.

♦ Have everyone count off by twos. Pass two baskets, labeled "one" and "two." All the "ones" put their card into the "one" basket, and "twos" do the same with their baskets. Pass the baskets a second time with all the "ones" taking a card from their basket, and "twos" doing the same with theirs.

Do It With Color

Audience size: more than 30

Materials:

♦ Three to five different colored 11-inch x 17-inch or larger poster boards

♦ 4-inch x 5-inch paper handouts, in the same colors as the posters

♦ Transparent tape

Objective: to get attendees to sit with people they do not know, thus immediately broadening their network

Time: throughout registration

Ahead of time, arrange the chairs in however many groups (different colors) you plan to use. Leave a little extra space between each group of chairs. Tape the 11-inch x 17-inch poster to the back of a chair in the last row so attendees can easily "spot" their color/section. Also presort the 4-inch x 5-inch pieces of paper, arranging all the colors in sequence so that two people who come together will not receive the same color.

As people arrive, hand them a color swatch at the door along with handouts (if any), directing them to their section. (If you are shorthanded, have the swatch lying on the registration table near a sign that says, "Take one. Sit in the appropriate section.")

This is a simple, effective way to get people to mix quickly. We used this technique at a relationship-building program sponsored by a public library. People responded willingly, and the pre-workshop din was evidence the technique was immediately successful.

2 + 2 = 4 or More

Audience size: any number of people standing or seated

Materials: blank card stock for those who don't have business cards

Objective: to encourage exchange of referrals

Time: 15-20 minutes

This is a good exercise to start an event in an interactive mode or to end on a positive note.

Ask people to have a business card handy. Then share the directions below.

1. Ask participants to introduce themselves to someone they do not know and use a few minutes to get acquainted.

2. Each pair then chooses another pair of people.

3. These four people exchange business cards.

4. Each person takes about a minute to tell the others about himself/herself.

5. Each individual tries to give one lead apiece to each of the other three people. The minimum objective is for everyone to get at least one lead. Leads can be warm (where they know the person and will allow their name to be used) or cold (they provide general, helpful information). Encourage participants to be assertive and follow up with their "foursomes" within a week.

Tom and Frank were part of a foursome at one of my networking programs. As I was cleaning up after the event, I noticed the two were still talking. As they left, they thanked me for making their meeting possible. They were going to continue their conversation at a restaurant next door and already had set up a luncheon meeting for the following week.

Variation

Have each member of the pair introduce his/her partner to the new pair they meet. Some people, especially Careful and Supportive networkers, find it easier to have someone else "toot their horn."

Find Your Mate
(Takeoff on 2 + 2 = 4 or More)

Audience size: 20 to 100s

Materials: pre-done "special" nametags for each attendee

Objective: to get people to mingle easily and get referrals (to be done during registration, with option to continue throughout program)

Time: 15-30 minutes

Ahead of time, put the complete name of one-half of a famous couple across the top third of a nametag. Leave the bottom two-thirds blank for the guest's name. If the audience is equally divided among men and women, give same sex tags to guests. If not, distribute names indiscriminately to men or women.

Tell people they need to find their well-known mate to complete their couple. Halfway thorough registration, announce that couples who have paired off must stay together until given permission to separate or divorce. (This helps break the ice and leads to more ingenious conversation and networking.)

When all the guests have arrived and "paired" off, ask each couple to get acquainted with another couple. Provide them with suggested conversation topics:

◆ How the pairs may have interacted had they really met

◆ How the couples would view the jobs held by attendees who bear their name

◆ How the couples might have networked when alive (when you choose couples from the past)

Also give each pair the option to talk about who they really are and their business. Suggest they exchange business cards.

When your program starts (if there is one), give couples the option of staying together, separating permanently or reuniting at break time.

Variations

Depending on the nature of your organization, you can choose different kinds of couples:

- Biblical
- Historical
- Modern-day
- Movies
- Musical
- Political
- Shakespearean
- Sports

For a media-connected event, you could choose:

- Books / authors
- DJs and stations
- Famous newspapers / founders
- News anchors / stations

Or how about famous sayings or greetings in different languages for intercultural events?

Let your creativity flow!

Networking Poker

Audience size: at least 40

Materials: enough playing cards (bridge cards) to equal guests

Objective: to have guests get acquainted by forming a human winning poker hand with two to four other people

Time: 20-30 minutes

Give each guest a playing card at registration along with a printed set of instructions. Modify the following instructions to meet your needs.

(Include the following on the instructions you hand out: *"Reprinted from Breakthrough Networking: Building Relationships That Last with permission of Duoforce Enterprises, Inc. 2003."*)

Networking Poker Instructions

1. You received one playing card at registration. Your goal is to join with two to four other guests to form a winning poker hand.

2. The winning hands in ascending order are:

   A. Two pairs

   B. Three-of-a-kind

   C. Straight (five cards in a row, different suit)

   D. Flush (any five cards, same suit)

   E. Straight flush (five cards in a row, same suit)

   F. Four-of-a-kind

   G. Royal flush (Ace, King, Queen, Jack, Ten—same suit)

3. You have until (set a time) to complete your hand; however, as soon as you think you have assembled a winning hand, check in at (designate a location). Until then, your objective is to assemble the top winning hand possible with the card you were given.

4. Once you have displayed a winning hand with your partners, you may not assemble another hand.

5. The highest value hand, using the order in (2), will win (name prize). Second prize for the next highest value hand will be (name prize). Third prize will be (name prize).

6. In case of ties, the first team checking in with that "hand" will be the winner.

Prizes can vary with your event and budget. You may choose to recognize from one winning hand to the top three or so, depending on number of attendees.

Networking Bingo

Audience size: more than 25 people

Materials:

- ◆ 8 1/2-inch x 11-inch pre-drawn Bingo card, preferably on heavy stock
- ◆ Pencils
- ◆ Blank card stock for those who do not have business cards
- ◆ Prize(s) for winner(s)

Objective: to use the popular game of Bingo to help guests mix and mingle

Time: 30 minutes

Variation I

1. Prepare a blank Bingo card entitled "Networking Bingo."

2. After most of the guests have arrived, hand out the cards and give oral instructions.

   A. Announce a time limit for the exercise.

   B. To complete the exercise, participants must have each box signed (or complete a vertical, horizontal, diagonal set of boxes) by a different person as well as have the person's business card or facsimile.

   C. Announce location where participants can present completed cards for verification.

D. In case of ties, you reserve the right to decide the winners.

E. Winners must present to the judge the person's business card for each signed square that qualifies.

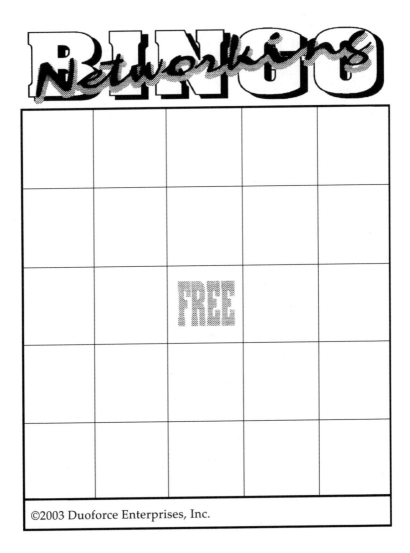

Variation II

1. Prepare a Bingo card entitled "Networking Bingo." Assign a business category chosen from pre-registrants to each square. Included might be:

Insurance	Accountant	Cosmetics	Financial Services	Therapist
Interior Designer	Attorney	Mortgage Lender	Advertising	Caterer
Cleaning Services	Printer	FREE	Marketing	Auto Sales
Travel Agent	Chiropractor	Landscaper	Florist	Ad Specialities
Realtor	Gift Baskets	Photographer	Optician	Artist

©2003 Duoforce Enterprises, Inc.

2. Follow instructions from Variation I except that participants must get each square signed by the guest who represents that business category.

3. Before you start, verify that all the categories in the card are present. If not, announce that "x" square is a freebie because that category is not present or choose a replacement business. Require a business card for each signed square.

Variation III

1. Prepare a Bingo card entitled "Networking Bingo." Assign a designation to each square that is relevant to your organization's gathering.

For instance, if you want to use this game to get guests and members mingling at a membership recruiting meeting of the American Association of University Women, use categories such as

Treasurer	Tall	Brown Hair	Entrepreneur	Member
Club President	Member	Company President	Club VP	Navy Blue Suit
Club Secretary	Blue Eyes	FREE	Guest	Glasses
Black Hair	Enthusiastic	October Birthday	Black Suit	Brown Eyes
Guest	Black Heels	Entrepreneur	Brown Hair	White Blouse

©2003 Duoforce Enterprises, Inc.

Again, require a business card to coincide with each completed square.

chapter 23

Workshop Exercises

The following exercises are designed to be used during workshops and conferences and may be adapted to your specific situation.

The Ever-Popular Handshake

Audience size: any size, seated

Materials: none; however, preferable if each person has business card

Objective: to encourage people to meet another person quickly and easily

Time: 5 minutes

This is an excellent exercise to get your audience involved in your presentation within the first minute or two and to get them acquainted with each other. It also gives those who have been sitting and waiting for the program an excuse to stand and stretch. To get the ball rolling, use opening remarks geared to your audience:

> *"Today, our goal is to get acquainted, and here's an exercise to start us on our way..."*

> *"I'm going to make sure that each of you meets at least one new person today..."*

> *"You're here to get better acquainted with others in your industry, and we're going to start right now ..."*

Ask each participant to have a business card handy. Then, ask everyone to stand and, beginning with rows 1, 3, 5, etc., ask alternate rows to turn around and give a power hand-shake to the person behind them. Ask them to get acquainted, making sure to exchange cards. Have people turn around because they tend to sit next to someone they already know, unless you divide them according to our "Do It With Color" exercise in Chapter 22.

> *Six months after I had led a marketing workshop, I received a call from Portia, one of the attendees. "Thanks for asking me to turn around," she said. She went on to tell me that not only has she become good friends with the woman she met through the exercise, she also had picked up three new clients for her financial planning business: the woman, her husband and her mother. "You made it so easy for me to do something that would have been awkward on my own," Portia added.*

I particularly like this exercise when I have a large audience. It can be done quickly, in an orderly fashion and accomplish good results.

Variation

You may choose to give each participant one of our **ICE BREAKERS** and have them use the questions to start the conversation. This will help them ease the fear of how to start a conversation with a stranger.

Changing Tables

Audience size: any size, seated

Materials: none

Objective: to help people meet a maximum amount of people within the constraints of your time and program

Time: 5 minutes

Event attendees tend to sit with people they know. This exercise allows participants to start off in their comfort zone and then encourages them to branch out as the program proceeds.

At break time or at lunch:

1. Ask participants to count off in threes and repeat the process until everyone has a number.

2. Ask all "ones" to stay where they are, while "twos" and "threes" change tables.

3. Depending on the size of the audience, you may wish to allow all the people to move at one time; have one side of the room change, then the other; the front half of the room, then the back.

Variation I

At break time, ask people on their own to find a new table with as many new faces as possible.

Variation II

At lunch, ask participants to find a new "partner" to connect with. If the group reassembles after lunch, ask them to "upset the fruit basket" once more as they take their materials and find a new seat.

52 Ways To Break The Ice & Target Your Market

Audience size: infinite

Materials: enough decks of **MARKET TARGETERS** to allow one per person

Objective: to help entrepreneurs through Fortune 100 employees refine marketing strategies and enhance their own and others' knowledge about their products and services

Time: preferably 10-15 minutes per person in groups of three or four

My experience has shown over and over that it is far easier to build a better mousetrap than it is to let the world know you have built a better one. Many small businesses fail because of lack of marketing expertise. Larger companies constantly strive to find the right marketing mix to increase sales and profits.

With the deck of 26 **MARKET TARGETERS,** you can help participants brainstorm and refine marketing information and strategies. An instructional manual offers suggestions for the facilitator/table leader to guide the discussion, as needed.

1. Divide participants into groups of three or four.

2. Choose someone to be "it" using the person whose birthday is nearest today or who is the newest employee.

3. "It" reads the question/statement on the card to the group. If introductions have not yet been officially made, it will be beneficial for the person to give a two-three minute introduction of self/business before seeking specific input.

4. The other participants will act as a business advisory council/focus group, helping "it" to come up with sound, creative approaches to his or her question/statement.

Variation I

All participants can use the same card throughout the exercise.

Variation II

Each person may choose a different targeted marketing situation (different card), again allowing 10-15 minutes per person.

Variation III

Each person may choose to do all cards over a scheduled period of time.

Variation IV

Participants can rotate tables, thereby enabling the process to be reenacted.

For more information, visit www.duoforce.com. An order form also is included at the end of this book.

Six Degrees of Separation

Audience size: any size, seated

Materials: none

Objective: to help prove the principle that everyone is just six people away from anyone in the world they want to meet or do business with

Time: 10-15 minutes

Explain that this exercise will show participants how simple it can be to get in contact with whomever they wish to meet as long as they are proactive and tell people what they want.

◆ If participants are seated around tables, let each one be a natural group. If seated theater style, divide them into groups of six to eight people,

◆ Use criteria, i.e., whoever's birthday is nearest the event, whoever traveled the farthest to get to the event, to select the first person to be "it."

◆ "It" shares with the group either

  • a person he/she wants to meet,

  • a person he/she wants to do business with,

  • a company he/she wants access to, or

  • a type of business (accounting, real estate) he/she wants to access.

◆ The rest of the people offer suggestions, general or specific, to help the person get nearer to her/his goal.

Variation

Tell the group they may elect to have two people be "it," with each taking a turn. If so, the other person might be the one who came in second in the criteria (birthday, travel) you chose.

Permission to Impersonate

Audience size: 12-15 people from the same company

Materials: a basket/container filled with each person's business card

Objective: to verify that co-workers or peers understand each other's responsibilities

Time: 20 minutes

◆ Make sure that all attendees have deposited one business card face down in the container you provided.

◆ Pass the basket to the right. Ask each person to take a card; make sure it is not his/her own and put it face down.

◆ Explain that all attendees will introduce themselves as if they are the person on the card. Ask them to give

  • their name,

  • their title and department,

  • description of their duties, and

  • any important tidbit about the other person.

Variation

(Another 20 Minutes)

Go around a second time and have people assume their own identities and share with the group one or two ways they can assist the person they introduced on the job (or give whatever assistance that may be in keeping with your organization).

This exercise has the twofold benefit of helping people see how well their job responsibilities are understood by others and of giving participants a chance to improve teamwork (if you also choose the variation).

It's an excellent "test" for groups that meet regularly to use periodically to see if members are clearly communicating what they do so others can introduce them accurately to their network.

Adjectives Say a Lot

Audience size: 12-15 people who have or haven't met before

Materials: none

Objective: to help attendees more easily remember each other's names

Time: 10–15 minutes

1. Ask each participant to think of an adjective that starts with the same letter as their first name and that best describes them a) personally or b) in the work place, depending on the occasion.

2. Explain that as facilitator you will start the exercise and then proceed around the room. In addition to his/her own adjective and name, each person must also name all the people who have preceded them—by adjective and name.

If your group is larger than 15, start the process over halfway through so people don't have an overwhelming number of adjectives/names to remember. My experience has been that people will recall others' names more easily and will remember them much longer when they have a descriptive word to attach to them.

Listen carefully to every person because you can gain valuable insight from the descriptors people use. Cautious Conrad usually is a Careful networking style. Sincere Susan probably indicates a Supportive style that is up front and honest. Marvelous Marla probably has high self-regard and isn't ashamed to say so. She's undoubtedly a Dauntless-Indefatigable style. Just Jenny may indicate someone who lacks self-esteem. This information is especially valuable to a trainer or facilitator as it gives you an overview of your audience from the participant's own perspective.

Variation

If your program permits, ask participants to use both the adjective and name throughout the day as they work with/call upon their comrades.

What's Your Brand?

Audience size: 5-20

Materials: enough notepad-size sheets of paper so each participant has one for all other participants

Objective: to help participants understand they have a brand, whether they have consciously created it or not

Time: 10-15 minutes

Explain that participants will take turns standing up, stating only their name. All of the others are to write the person's name on a piece of paper and then two or three words to describe the person based on looking at them. Ask those sitting to fold their paper once or twice and then pass it to the person who has been standing. That person now sits down and participates in the rest of the exercise.

All papers are to remain folded until everyone has had a turn, after which participants may look at what others see as their brand.

Debrief the group as a whole, particularly if you have a small number. Divide larger groups into pairs to discuss their reactions to what others saw. They may also choose to seek further input from their partner.

Find Common Ground

Audience size: any size, seated

Materials: none

Objective: to help strangers/casual acquaintances to find commonalties and stimulate the relationship-building process

Time: 10 minutes

This exercise works well as part of a relationship-building talk to civic, professional or service groups or day-long training programs and workshops.

Lay the groundwork by discussing how people feel most comfortable with people with whom they share commonalties. Explain that people who have just met (or know each other casually) often have more in common than they might imagine. You will help them with the discovery process.

1. Pair off people or if group is larger, divide into smaller groups of four.

2. Give participants a broad topic or if you want to challenge them even more, specific areas within the topic.

   ◆ Holidays: family traditions/favorite memory

   ◆ Vacations: most memorable/longest/most exciting

   ◆ Childhood: favorite memory/favorite grandparent chores

   ◆ School: favorite subject/most memorable year/what you would do differently

3. Give them five minutes to establish a commonality within the group.

4. Have the groups report back about methods they used to find a commonality and how easy/hard it was to do so.

5. Ask participants how they will use the principles they learned in real-life relationship-building situations.

Variation

Divide the participants and ask them to find a commonality without any help on your part. Repeat steps 3, 4 and 5.

Notes

1. Mather, Cotton. *Manuductio Ad Ministerium*. Boston, Mass., 1726.

2. Pool, Ithiel de Sola, and Manfred Kochen. "Contacts and Influence," *Social Contacts*, 1978–1979.

3. Carnes, Barbara. "The History of DiSC: It's Older Than You Think." Minneapolis, Minn.: Carlson Learning Company Network Magazine, January 1990.

4. Jung, C.M. *Psychological Types*. Princeton, N.J.: Princeton University Press, 1971. A revision by R.F.C. Hill of the translation by H.G. Baynes.

5. Marston, William Moulton. *The Emotions of Normal People*. Condensed version 1987. First published in 1978 by Persona Press, Inc., Minneapolis, MN.

6. Thompson, Jacqueline. *Image Impact*. New York: Arrowood Press, 1990. (William Thourlby was a contributing editor.)

7. Wagner, Carlton. *Let Your Colors Do the Talking*. Wagner Institute for Color Research, 1985.

8. Mehrabian, A. *Silent Messages: Implicit Communication of Emotions & Attitudes*. Belmont, Calif.: Wadsworth Publishing, 1981.

9. Hall, E.T. *The Hidden Dimensions*. New York: Doubleday & Co., 1966.

10. Lewis, David. *The Secret Language of Success*. New York: Carroll & Graf Publishers, 1990.

11. Wallechinsky, David. *The People's Almanac Presents the Book of Lists*. New York: Morrow, 1977.

12. Tannen, Deborah. *That's Not What I Meant*. New York: William Morrow and Company, 1986.

13. Maltz, Mawell. *Psycho-Cybernatics*. New York: Pocket Books, 1960.

Communicate and Network Your Way to Success
Learning Tools From Duoforce Enterprises, Inc.

**Please mail to Duoforce Enterprises, 2221 Ridgewood Rd., PO Box 1154, Lisle, IL 60532
Fax to 630-983-5312 or order from www.duoforce.com**

Breakthrough Networking:
Building Relationships That Last . . . . _____ *books* @ $21.95/book_____

52 Ways To Break The Ice & Target Your Market
(Includes 1 deck each of **ICE BREAKERS** and
MARKET TARGETERS with instructional manual)
Complete package: . . . . ._____ *sets* @ $98.00 each_____

ICE BREAKERS *only* (26 cards)
1-4 decks: . . . . ._____ *decks* @ *$26/apiece*_____
5-8 decks: . . . . ._____ *decks* @ *$23/apiece*_____
9 or more: . . . . ._____ *decks* @ *$20/apiece*_____

MARKET TARGETERS *only* (26 cards)
1-4 decks: . . . . ._____ *decks* @ *$26/apiece*_____
5-8 decks: . . . . ._____ *decks* @ *$23/apiece*_____
9 or more: . . . . ._____ *decks* @ *$20/apiece*_____

Personal Profile System   @ $15.50   _____
Personalized Communication Report   @ $98.00   _____

Nothing Happens Until We Communicate
This comprehensive series shows/tells you how you communicate through appearance, body language, gender, listening, presentation, self-esteem and writing skills. *(Circle the specific one[s] you want.)*

Nothing Happens Until We Communicate Tapes/Workbooks
   * *Don't Wait Another 10 Seconds*   * *Unlock Your Potential Within*
   * *Speak Easy: Overcome the Number One Fear* * *We Say It Without Words*
   * *Sssh! Listen, Don't Just Hear*   * *Write Right*

Tapes only
   * *He Said/She Said - Business*   * *He Said/She Said - Personal*
Single workbook: . . . . ._____ *books* @ $14.95   _____
Single audiotape: . . . . ._____ *tapes* @ $9.80   _____
6 workbook series: . . . . ._____ *sets* @ $74.75   _____
8 audiotape series: . . . . ._____ *sets* @ $68.60   _____

To order

Name _____ Title_____

Company Name _____

Address_____

City_____ State _____ Zip_____

Business Phone _____ E-mail _____

Payment Form

Check [   ]   ❏ VISA ❏ Mastercard   Credit Card Expiration Date_____

Credit Card #_____   3 number V-Code from back of card _____

Name on card _____ Signature _____

Amount Enclosed

Subtotal from above . . . . _____

Sales Tax
Illinois residents add 6.75% . . . . ._____

Shipping and Handling
52 Ways To Break The Ice & Target Your Market, $9.80 for first one.
Additional packages, $5. For all other items, $4.50 for the first; $1.50
for each additional item. Contact lillian@duoforce.com for Canadian
or overseas shipping and handling charges. Allow 30 days delivery. . . . . ._____

Total: . . . . _____